HEROIC, HELPFUL, & CARING CATS

Felines Who Make a Difference

REVISED

Anne E. Beall, PhD

HEROIC, HELPFUL, & CARING CATS: Felines Who Make a Difference

Copyright © 2022 by Anne Beall/Beall Research, Inc.

Originally published in 2020 and Revised 2022

All rights reserved. No part of this book may be reproduced in any form or by any electronic or mechanical means, including information storage and retrieval systems, without permission in writing from the author. The only exception is by a reviewer, who may quote short excerpts in a review.

Cover Designed by Atiq Ahmed with image from Obrik/stock.adobe.com

ISBN: 97989858884-6-1 (paperback)
ISBN: 97989858884-7-8 (hardcover)

Time spent with cats is never wasted.
          SIGMUND FREUD

There are two means of refuge from the miseries of life: music and cats.
          ALBERT SCHWEITZER

What greater gift than the love of a cat.

          CHARLES DICKENS

For all the people who save, foster, and care for cats: you are the most compassionate and the best example of our humanity.

And in memory of Sarina Beana Beall, who spent twenty-one years of her life with me. You are sorely missed, my sweet cat.

Contents

Tables 3

Figures 5

Foreword 6

Preface 11

Acknowledgments 13

Chapter 1: Heroic Henry, The Lost Cat Finder 15

Chapter 2: GG, The Career Counselor 20

Chapter 3: Pearl, Breaking Down Barriers to Do Therapy in Hospitals 24

Chapter 4: Lola, A Dumpster Cat, Creates A Writer 29

Chapter 5: Rascal, The Cat Who Consoled and Gave Courage for A New Life 33

Chapter 6: Peach, Pushing the Boundaries of What We Believe Cats Can Do 37

Chapter 7: Community Cats Create a Fighter 42

Chapter 8: Belle, Healing Attendant 47

Chapter 9: Tommy, Educating Us About Special Needs 51

Chapter 10: Zack, Socializer & Calming Influence for an Anxious Teenager 55

Chapter 11: Community Cats Bring People Together 59

Chapter 12: Tino, the Intuitive Feline Therapist 63

Chapter 13: July, Simply an Angel 68

Chapter 14: Basil, A Calming Influence Wherever She Goes 71

Chapter 15: Moe Grey, Educator and Celebrity Ambassador 75

Chapter 16: Nuala, Patient and Compassionate Healer 78

Chapter 17: Four Kittens Teach About Animal Advocacy and Courage 82

Chapter 18: Community Cats Create a Fierce Advocate Named Rae 86

Chapter 19: Ayla and Buddy, Life Coaches 91

Chapter 20: Survey of How Cats Help Americans and Prevalent Attitudes 94

Anne E. Beall, PhD. 120

Steve Dale 121

End Notes 122

Tables

Table 1: Current pets in the home 95
Table 2: Number of cats currently in the household 95
Table 3: Number of cats that respondents have had as an adult 95
Table 4: Hours spent each day with cat 100
Table 5: How the caretaker has helped cat 101
Table 6: How cat has helped caretaker 102
Table 7: Feelings about cat 103
Table 8: Average number and percentage of indoor cats 104
Table 9: Average number and percentage of outdoor cats 105
Table 10: Feral cat colony that is regularly fed 105
Table 11: Number of cats in colony 106
Table 12: Amount spent feeding colony cats per month 106
Table 13: Reasons caretaker started taking care of stray cats 107
Table 14: Whether caretaker has been harassed 107
Table 15: Feelings about stray cats 108
Table 16: Actions toward stray cats 108
Table 17: Actions toward stray cat that will die in two years 109
Table 18: Attitudes toward euthanizing cats in shelters 109
Table 19: Knowledge of Trap-Neuter-Return programs 111
Table 20: Information about TNR programs 112
Table 21: Most important information about TNR programs 113
Table 22: Believability of information about TNR programs 115
Table 23: Age of respondents 117
Table 24: Gender of respondents 117
Table 25: Race/ethnicity of respondents 117
Table 26: Annual household income of respondents 118

Table 27: Region of the country where respondents lived 118
Table 28: Number of children living at home 119
Table 29: Area where respondent lived... 119

Figures

Figure 1: Intelligence of cat compared to other animals (n=3,169) 96
Figure 2: Intelligence of cat compared to humans (n=3,169) 97
Figure 3: Amount of communication between caretaker & cat (n=3,169)..........98
Figure 4: How well the cat reads the caretaker (n=3,169) 98
Figure 5: How well caretaker reads the cat (n=3,169) 99
Figure 6: How close the caretaker feels to cat (n=3,169)................................100
Figure 7: How respondents view TNR programs (n=1,507)............................111
Figure 8: How respondents feel about TNR after information (n=1,507)..........114
Figure 9: How likely to support a free TNR program (n=1,507) 116
Figure 10: How likely to become a colony caretaker (n=1,388).......................116

Foreword

I'm guilty, or at least I was guilty. Like so many people who had never been previously owned by a cat, I had misconceptions about the behavior of domestic cats.

Just between us, here's the sad truth: I thought dogs were more connected to people, and frankly the brainier species.

This tragic miscalculation wasn't totally my fault. The problem is that I am human. As a human, I'm more predisposed to understand canines. After all, our species co-evolved with dogs. Dating back over 40,000 years Cro-Magnon men (and women) began to domesticate a wolf species, now long extinct.

Even back then, humanoids would partner on hunts with the developing species (we now call dogs), and we shared sleeping space, as they trusted us with their cubs, and we trusted them with our newborns. Often humans were buried with their dogs. The alliance is a one of a kind in the animal kingdom. And over time, we continued to selectively breed dogs for desired traits.

The feline story is far more recent, and far simpler. Feline domestication took place about five to eight thousand years ago simultaneously in several places on the planet. Although humans actively and thoughtfully domesticated dogs, cats decided on their own that living near humans might be a good deal. While hanging out where we grew crops, cats enjoyed an abundance of vermin. Clearly, it was also a good deal for humans. But humans didn't need to teach cats this skill, and they never really worked together with cats as they did dogs.

Of course, the relationship with cats has developed over time. But along the way, cats have alternatively been revered and reviled. I'll offer an example of each: In ancient Egypt cats were revered as a representative of a Goddess. In fact, Bastet was the Egyptian cat Goddess of the home, domesticity, women's secrets, fertility, and childbirth. She protected the home from evil spirits and disease, especially diseases associated with women and children.

The Black Death, one of the most devastating pandemics in human history, spread across Europe between 1346 and 1353, and for many years cats were blamed and persecuted as a result. It is widely believed that the plague was caused by the bacterium *Yersinia pestis* commonly present in populations of fleas carried by rodents. Religious and political leaders of the day blamed the plague on witchcraft and evil cats, whom they ordered to be killed. No surprise, the rat population burgeoned where cats were decimated.

And all these years later, it seems, beliefs about cats have not changed. People either love them or they don't. I argue, (and there is some science to demonstrate), that unless you've had a bad experience with a dog, you generally are going to like dogs.

So maybe not loving or understanding cats isn't completely our fault.

I never shared my life with a cat, until I met Ricky.

Ricky was a handsome stark white Devon Rex kitten, who loved people. The breeder, Leslie Spiller, did a great job of giving him positive encounters with strangers from a young age, and my wife Robin and I continued that process.

Not only did Ricky enjoy when people visited, he often smothered our guests with love, hopping on to unsuspecting friend's shoulders and purring into their ears.

One day my wife, Robin, returned from an animal assisted therapy session with our Miniature Australian Shepherd, Lucy. She said, "teach Lucy a new trick." Lucy knew lots of parlor tricks, even singing a song to kids at the Rehabilitation Institute of Chicago. So, I thought I could teach her to play a little kid's piano.

I closed the door of our "training room," (a second bedroom) and began the process of clicker training Lucy. I started to shape the behavior, the closer her paw came to the keyboard, I would click a clicker and offer a treat. Gradually it was working. After all, you can't instantly train a composer.

Or maybe you can.

It turned out, I didn't close the door all the way, and Ricky ambled into the "training room." He looked at me, looked at the dog, and proceeded to play the piano. No clicker. No treat. Nothing. But I quickly began to reinforce my prodigy.

Here's the truth: He trained me to train him. And it wasn't long before Ricky was offering high fives, literally jumping through hoops, and jumping over dogs. People were amazed.

How can a cat do this?

Ricky began appearing at recitals in local pet stores, and he appeared on many national TV shows, from *Animal Planet* and *National Geographic* shows to public television.

Ricky taught me and taught millions of people what cats are capable of. And our bond was palpable. If I had fallen into a well, like Lassie, Ricky would have rescued me. We were inseparable.

I believe in twice yearly veterinary exams, and we scheduled what was supposed to be a routine exam.

As per my veterinarian's request, Ricky performed a few of his improvisational jazz tunes for the staff and clients who happened to be there with their dogs – all crowded into a little exam room. After the applause (a standing ovation as there were no seats in the room), Dr. Donna Solomon began the exam by listening to Ricky's heart. Her face told me the story. She heard a murmur. A veterinary cardiologist, Dr. Michael Luethy, confirmed Ricky had feline hypertrophic cardiomyopathy (HCM), an abnormal thickening of the heart. Although medication may slow the disease progress– nothing more could be done. Some cats diagnosed with HCM do live out a normal life. However, most do not.

Happily, Ricky never read the prognosis, and probably felt well until his final months. As his celebrity status grew, I even turned down a bit for David Letterman's 'Stupid Pet Tricks' because I wouldn't fly with Ricky to New York City or drive there from Chicago.

Ricky was only four and one-half years old when he suddenly succumbed to HCM in 2002. He just collapsed. I still remember that point in time as if it was yesterday.

HCM might be the most common cause of death of cats from about three to ten years. How could such a common disease have no effective treatment?

I partnered with the Winn Feline Foundation–a non-profit funder of cat health studies–and created the Ricky Fund to raise money for HCM research. Today, we've raised well over $250,000.

The good news is that with those dollars a genetic test was created to determine if a gene defect for HCM occurs in Maine Coon and Ragdoll cats. Breeders implementing the simple and inexpensive test in their breeding programs have saved lives.

Ricky's chronicles could easily fill two books. Here's my favorite:

If Garth Brooks could perform in Central Park, I thought Ricky could play piano on the front steps of our condo building. At one such outdoor concert, Billy, a ten-year old boy with Down's syndrome, walked by. He was enthralled. He stared at Ricky for several minutes, and then spontaneously began to giggle. We're not talking little giggles here. I mean full blown belly laughter.

Just then, Billy, who was still in stitches, began to pet Ricky. Then Billy sat down and snuggled with Ricky, now purring in his lap. I don't know what secrets Billy shared, but he whispered to Ricky for several minutes. Just before he and his mom departed, Billy looked at Ricky and said, "I love you," and then he kissed Ricky.

His mother had tears streaming down her face and quietly said, "Billy's father passed on two weeks ago. Everyone tried to get him to talk, to react. Thank you."

Indeed, cats can be heroic, helpful, and caring.

Steve Dale, CABC

Ricky at the piano
(Photo courtesy of Steve Dale)

Preface

Some people say cats are aloof and detached. Although cats may not be as exuberant as dogs, they're clearly connected to the humans around them. In fact, researchers have found cats have attachment styles very similar to humans[i]. Attachment theory posits that early in life, people have one of four attachment styles: secure, ambivalent, avoidant, or disorganized. Those who are securely attached are comforted by their caretaker's presence, whereas those who are ambivalent tend to be clingy and overdependent. Those who are avoidant seem disinterested, whereas those who are disorganized have a combination of styles. Researchers have found that sixty-four percent of cats have a secure attachment to their caretakers. Roughly thirty percent are ambivalent, and the rest (six percent) are avoidant. These findings mirror those of humans and other animals, including dogs.

I have had a strong connection with every cat who has been in my life. Sarina Beana was the cat who was with me the longest—she was twenty-one years old when she passed away. During a terrible fight with my ex-spouse, she heard me yelling loudly and crying. She came out of the bedroom, jumped on the couch, and rubbed her face against mine. She was clearly trying to comfort me. She was with me through good and bad times, my rock for many years.

I've also fostered several cats over the years and discovered that even those who have been abused or neglected can bond with us and teach us valuable lessons. One cat, Ginger, had been homeless for ten years and came to me with dirty, matted fur. He was scrawny and had not been eating well. I imagine that if I'd been living in these terrible conditions for so long, I'd be bitter. He wasn't. He taught me that forgiveness is essential, and that you must make the most of every moment. His life had been hard, and yet he was the kindest creature I've ever met. He greeted me with enthusiasm every time I went into his space. He was with me for nine months and only ever showed me patience and kindness.

As I was writing this book, I saw many examples of how cats connect with people. One day, I spied a homeless man sitting on Michigan Avenue with a pet cat who was wearing a harness. I stopped to talk to him about his cat. He told me that he struggled with mental illness and that the cat has helped him deal with life on the streets. The cat sensed when he was having a panic attack and would sit right next to him during his roughest hours. The cat was well-fed and cared for, and it was obvious they had a strong bond that transcended their living conditions.

I became interested in the types of relationships cats have with their caretakers in the average household, so my firm conducted survey research among Americans who have had cats in their lives; it is shared in the last chapter. The average person has been greatly affected by their cat(s). They view these cats as highly intelligent and able to read their caretaker's feelings and preferences, and they help their caretaker in many ways. One thing I learned is that cats make the person feel happy and unconditionally loved. What a tremendous gift.

I've long believed cats make a huge difference in the lives of those around them, so I collected stories from people who felt their felines had changed their lives. I wanted to share these tales to show that cats care about people and don't just regard them as an avenue to get their next meal. But I also wanted to share them because they personally moved me and changed how I look at cats.

-Anne E. Beall, Chicago

Acknowledgments

I would like to thank the many people who shared their stories with me and gave me a glimpse into their lives. Many opened themselves up and told me their deepest feelings, some told me intimate details. They painted vivid portraits of the cats in their lives, what they had learned, and how these creatures had changed them.

I also want to thank my colleagues at Beall Research, who helped me to write and field the survey that's included in the final chapter of this book. Thanks to Mark Geniesse and Cathy Noji, who gave valuable feedback on the structure and content of the survey. Thanks also to Gina Butterfield, who managed the fielding of the study and who ensured quotas were met and data-quality standards were in place. Another person to thank is Mike Karlinski, who tabulated the data in many ways to give insights into Americans' experiences and attitudes toward cats.

I'd also like to thank Pet Partners and specifically Mary Margaret Callahan, who connected me with individuals who have cats certified as therapy animals. These cats make a difference in many places—hospitals, schools, and community spaces.

A thanks also to Lauren Miele, who invited me to the Meow Meetup in Chicago and who encouraged me to seek out stories about cats from conference attendees. Many of the people in this book were individuals I met at that conference who told me touching stories.

I'd also like to thank Diane Telgen, who meticulously edited this book with great enthusiasm, and turned my writing into elegant prose. If the book is easy to read, it's because of her.

I'd also like to thank Christine Holt and Judi Goshen, who proofread the final version of this manuscript and brought it close to perfection.

And last, I'd like to thank Steve Dale, who is a tireless supporter of my work and who is a tremendous animal advocate. He wrote the Foreword and has always known how much animals bring to our lives. Many animals all over the world have been helped by his tireless advocacy.

Chapter 1: Heroic Henry, The Lost Cat Finder

Kimberley Freeman is an animal whisperer. She communicates with animals at a completely different level through understanding how each species views their world. She uses this insight to great advantage; she's trained cats, horses, and even squirrels. When she discovered how clicker training transformed the relationship with her horse, she tried it with shelter cats to help them be more social. As a result, the adoption rate at the shelter where she worked tripled.

Kimberley's understanding of feline psychology has made her an expert in finding lost cats. Over the years, she's found hundreds of cats on her own, but always wanted an animal partner to help her with tracking. She realized a dog would scare cats away, but a friendly cat might be able to track another cat without causing panic and alarm. However, she knew it would have to be a very special feline.

In 2013, Kimberley was attending an outdoor adoption event featuring Jackson Galaxy. He invited local shelters to bring adoptable pets who needed homes. As she wandered the grounds, Kimberley spotted a black and white tuxedo cat in a harness lounging on a grassy hill. The cat watched calmly as dogs went by, kids ran around yelling, and random strangers stopped to talk with him. This cat was so chill and unfazed by the chaos, Kimberley had to meet him. The shelter group told her he was ten years old and had been at the shelter for over a year. There was something unique about this tuxedo cat, so she asked to take him for a walk to test his interest in scent and unfamiliar places. He remained calm, curious, and fearless, both in wide open spaces and tight dark areas. Despite his age, she felt sure she'd found the ideal cat who could partner with her to find lost cats.

Lost Cats!

Kimberley started training Henry at their Texas ranch, and he quickly learned how to follow a scent trail. Within one month, he tracked a stray cat and proved his talent at home, but what about in the real world? It wasn't long before his skills would be called upon by a woman who had lost her orange cat, Ruby.

Ruby got out when her caretaker, Anne Marie, came in from a trip to the grocery store. Anne Marie searched the neighborhood with no luck, so she contacted Kimberley. The lost-cat team rushed over to their Austin home. Henry sniffed a couch cushion Ruby slept on and headed out the door. He sniffed all around the garage, then went under Anne Marie's Chevy Suburban and lay down. Kimberley was perplexed about why he quit working. Was it because of the summer heat? She coaxed him out to try to pick up a trail through the neighborhood. Henry was curious, but not engaged. When they went back to Anne Marie's house, it occurred to Kimberley that maybe Henry was trying to tell her something. When she shimmied under the vehicle's carriage, she spotted three orange hairs caught on the crossbars. Ruby had been up in the vehicle but was no longer there.

Kimberley deduced the cat may have been on the underside of the vehicle when Anne Marie drove to the gym, so they put posters at every intersection along the way. It wasn't long before a man contacted them. He saw Ruby when the Suburban hit the brakes. The cat fell out of the car, almost got hit by another car, and then ran into a residential neighborhood. Near that intersection, Kimberley found Ruby hiding in a garage that had a small gap under the door.

Anne Marie was ecstatic to be reunited with Ruby. A trip to the vet the next day revealed Ruby had only a minor scrape on her shoulder: no broken bones or major injuries. Kimberley realized Henry had done his job well and resolved to pay closer attention to what he was telling her during their tracking work.

Henry's next job was saving Mo, a 6-month-old kitten who disappeared when his family moved across the country. The family stopped at a gas station late at night and did not see Mo slip out the car door. Arriving at their new home four hours later, they realized Mo was missing and figured it must have occurred at the gas station. They called a shelter who recommended Kimberley and Henry. You can see Henry working this case on YouTube under "Search & Rescue Cat Finds Lost Kitten" with Henry in his orange vest heading toward a deck. There were many places to hide, but within minutes, Henry found Mo and they called the owners with the good news.

Another cat Henry rescued was a deaf kitty named Violet. Her caretakers, Tracie and Tobin, went on vacation and left their cats with a pet sitter. When they returned, Violet was missing. They searched everywhere for days. Because Violet couldn't hear them calling her, they were even more worried, especially with so many neighbors warning about coyotes in the area. They were desperate but dubious when they called Kimberley. Although Violet had been gone for nine days, Henry came out and tracked her to a shed down the street where she was hiding in terror. Tracie and Tobin rushed to the scene with a carrier, overjoyed to be reunited with a trembling Violet, wishing they had contacted the Lost Cat Finder team sooner.

A Great Sense of Humor

Henry and Kimberley had such an amazing partnership that he could sense when she was having a rough day and start his comedy show. Henry would sneak up, hide behind the sofa, and then jump up in the air with a look on his face as if he was saying, "gotcha!" Or he would flop down at her feet and flip upside down, knowing the view of his fluffy tummy would make her smile. As she explained, "he wasn't just my working partner, he was my comic relief."

To practice their tracking, Henry and Kimberley would head down to the creek each morning, where he sniffed around to see what animals had been by the previous night. When he smelled something new, his eyes got big and he'd look up at Kimberley as if to say, "do you smell that? Can you believe it?" He kept her constantly entertained with his antics, facial expressions, and calm way of dealing with the world.

Pet sitters and others who met Henry often commented on how friendly, fearless, and social he was. Whenever workers would come to the house for a project, Henry would march right up to see what they were doing. The workers often remarked he was like a dog in a cat suit. In one of his "Cat with a Camera" TikTok videos, you can see Henry's POV as he walks up to a poodle in a pink harness just to say hello. Henry was truly fearless and saw the world as a place full of opportunities to meet and greet.

A Lasting Legacy

Henry retired from his tracking job in 2020 when he was nearly twenty years old. He worked until Kimberley was no longer comfortable putting him into unfamiliar situations. When Henry was diagnosed with kidney disease and became unsteady walking, Kimberley carried him down to the creek in his favorite woven basket so he could enjoy the outdoor sights and sounds he loved so much. A few months later, he passed away.

Kimberley says Henry taught her many things during their partnership. He taught her to slow down and focus, to learn the value of taking your time and being in the present moment. Although there is a deep hole in her soul from his absence, she says the memories of the relationship they shared along with his lasting love and lessons console her every day.

Henry was truly a heroic cat.

Henry and Kimberley (Photo courtesy of Kimberley Freeman)

Chapter 2: GG, The Career Counselor

When GG came into Trevor and Launa Enberg's life in 2016, they had no idea how much she would change their lives. They brought the tortoiseshell cat home after seeing an advertisement about kittens for sale. They had been unable to find any kittens at the local SPCA, shelters, and rescue associations, which they found surprising. They had always been pet people, with three previous cats and a dog who lived until old age. They missed having an animal at home, and it seemed like the right time. As a veterinarian who works as an emergency and critical-care specialist, Trevor is no stranger to cats. That first night, Launa noticed the kitten was listless, weak, and limp. Although they thought the kitten was eating, she was just moving food around because she was so young, she hadn't learned how to eat solid food yet. Trevor immediately took her to his veterinary hospital in the middle of the night and gave her fluids, a dextrose solution, and antibiotics. He did everything he could to save the kitten. As he worked, he thought, *I'd better not mess this up. If I can't save my own cat, how can I save others? And how will I face Launa?*

The kitten rallied and Trevor brought her home, where they fed her every couple of hours with a syringe for the next two weeks. Launa would also wipe her backside to stimulate her to urinate and defecate, just like a mother cat would do. It was obvious that GG was only a few weeks old when they got her and not the age the sellers stated. The little kitten needed attention twenty-four hours a day, but eventually began to eat and use the litter box on her own.

Trevor Pays a Price for his Profession

Launa and Trevor named their kitten GG, for the airport code of their favorite holiday site, Maui (OGG), and she quickly became an important member of the family. The couple didn't have kids by choice, and they viewed her as their child. And GG may have even viewed herself that way. From her early days with them, she would climb up into their laps or lie next to their faces and suck the fur between the toes of her paw. She would make a sweet burbling noise, which showed how much comfort their presence gave her. And because she was so young and needed to be fed frequently, they took her everywhere. They also dressed her in different clothing, which she didn't seem to mind because the apparel enveloped her and made her feel secure. Trevor thinks her tolerance for dresses started because she wore a body harness inside her carriers, so she got used to having something that surrounded her.

But GG became more than just a child substitute; she helped Trevor during his darkest days. Emergency and critical-care veterinarians have one of the toughest jobs in the industry. Trevor has been a veterinarian for twenty-six years, but the last seventeen have been spent in critical care. In that area, it's normal to lose roughly one-quarter of all patients. He used to keep track of the number of animals he lost, but he gave up after twelve years because he couldn't change the mortality rate.

There is a tremendous amount of stress and anxiety associated with taking care of critically ill animals. Each day, Trevor deals with animals in life-threatening situations: those who have been hit by cars; others who have ingested garbage, poisons, or foreign objects; and animals with organ failure (liver, kidney or heart) or neurological issues (e.g., seizures, paralysis). It's difficult to watch animals die that you can't save and even more difficult to comfort the companions, who are often inconsolable, or who sometimes want to keep a pet alive longer than what's in the best interest of the animal.

All these issues took a toll on Trevor, who coped by building up an emotional shield that made him somewhat detached and cold in his job. He basically came to feel nothing in order to function. It's called "compassion fatigue," and it's rampant in helping professions. Trevor eventually became so detached that he enjoyed nothing and felt neither joy nor sadness.

GG Helps Trevor

As she grew up and became a part of the family, GG somehow managed to penetrate Trevor's emotional detachment. He explained, "she softened me and removed the armor around my heart." GG reminded Trevor what it was like to be attached to an animal and how fulfilling it is to have a cat wait for you to get home, greet you, snuggle with you, and want to go everywhere with you. GG showed Trevor how much she loved him. As he progressively became more detached from his profession, GG began to pay more attention to him. Neither he nor Launa understood what was happening. She seemed to know that he needed this attention and helped him realize what was happening for him emotionally. Trevor finally faced the emotional crisis that had been building for several years. He broke down and took time off from work, got counseling, and started to deal with the realities of being a veterinarian in emergency and critical-care services.

GG helped Trevor by giving him love and time to heal without any pressure. She seemed to understand that he needed comfort. Her presence calmed Trevor and allowed him to let go of the pain he was holding inside. Being able to save GG and having her constant love helped him deal with his emotions about the animals he couldn't help. No matter how bereft Trevor felt, GG was always there and always wanted to spend time with him. "She let me address my crisis—she was the emotional therapy I needed because she helped me get in touch with my feelings and made it safe to do so," he said.

Trevor believes GG saved his career and current life because she helped him to feel again and to deal with the emotions from his work. "The combination of counseling, Launa's support, and time with GG is what allowed me to go back to work," he said. And GG continues to help him. "Sometimes when I have a really tough day at work, I text Launa and ask her to find GG and squeeze her for me." Trevor will return from work and find his cute tortoiseshell cat waiting for him, eager to spend some quality time together. It's the best salve for any emotional upset from the day.

GG Goes Everywhere

GG is an exceptional cat by any measure. At this point, her bond is so strong with Launa and Trevor that she travels everywhere with them. She's been on a boat, a ferry, a train, the city bus, the city SkyTrain, airplanes, and a float plane. She's flown twenty-six times! (Too bad airlines don't give frequent-flyer miles to cats.) GG loves to be with Launa and Trevor so much that she apparently doesn't mind being in a carrier—or even donning a cat-sized life vest when on a boat. And unlike many cats, she always likes to be picked up and held. It's not surprising that Trevor's professional veterinarian photo on his organization's website features a picture of himself with GG.

Eventually Trevor honored GG by having a tattoo of her put on his calf. The tattoo is a great way to honor the cat who saved his career and his life, and who is always there to help him overcome a bad day.

Trevor and GG (Photo courtesy of Trevor Enberg)

Chapter 3: Pearl, Breaking Down Barriers to Do Therapy in Hospitals

Although many cats help their owners cope with their troubles, some special individuals spread comfort to everyone they meet. That is certainly the case with Pearl, a five-year old grey Burmese therapy cat. But getting a therapy cat into a hospital is no easy task, according to Geralyn Hawk. However, she and Pearl persisted in their fight to be an important part of the healing process for pediatric patients at the University Hospital of Cleveland. Geralyn had been going to the hospital for years with her therapy dogs, but she felt some patients would love the kind of therapy a cat could provide. However, the hospital never had a cat in their animal-therapy program, so they said no.

Pearl Can Handle Anything

Pearl is one of only 222 cats who have been certified as therapy animals through Pet Partners, (which is one of the largest organizations that certifies therapy animals, with over 13,000 human-animal therapy teams[ii]). Therapy dogs and horses are most common—there are currently 10,000 dogs and 400 horses certified through this organization. Pearl was the right cat to take on the challenge of getting into a hospital because she loves going to new places. When Geralyn gets her cat's stroller or carrier out, Pearl gets excited. She likes riding in cars and going places. Pearl can handle busy, loud situations that most cats would find distressing. Pearl also likes meeting new people. When people visit her home, Pearl always goes over to greet and interact with them. She's like a dog, according to Geralyn.

Pearl's therapy work began in a nursing home, where she was a hit; the residents adored her. Then Pearl went to Case Western Reserve University, where she was swarmed by college kids during exam week. The students were stressed about their grades and needed a break from studying. Pearl visited with the kids in the university's main library. When Geralyn told the hospital about Pearl's impressive abilities, the hospital was unmoved.

Pearl continued to push the boundaries when she became involved in an "After Prom" event that John Carroll University held for developmentally disabled teenagers who attended their week-long camp. The event had a DJ, a large slide, and a popcorn machine in a large grassy area. Teens were running around, and the music was loud. Geralyn was concerned that Pearl would be overwhelmed and stressed, and she brought a carrier where the cat could retreat. But the opposite occurred; Geralyn walked around with Pearl on a harness and leash for two hours. Pearl walked up to many different people, interacted with dogs, and had a great time.

Getting Accepted, Finally!

Geralyn brought these examples to the hospital management and explained that Pearl could handle the hospital environment and would make a difference there. She described the many situations where Pearl had shown her mettle. But still the answer was no.

When Geralyn would visit the hospital with her therapy dogs, she would sometimes give Pearl's picture to patients. Many of these people wanted a cat to visit them, but Geralyn explained that cats were not a part of the therapy program. Patients began asking hospital management to allow cats to provide therapy. Apparently, the demand for Pearl became clamorous. And in March of 2018, Pearl was finally accepted as part of the animal-therapy program.

Pearl must meet the same requirements that are applied to therapy dogs. She is bathed regularly, and Geralyn applies a dose of Allerpet, which reduces dander, before every visit. When Geralyn goes into a hospital room, she puts down a towel or sheet to form a barrier between Pearl and the hospital bedding, so that no hair or dander is left behind. Geralyn also wipes Pearl's paws with a disinfectant wipe before the visit and then each patient is given a disinfectant wipe afterward. Geralyn also uses hand sanitizer on her own hands before every new visit.

Little Miracles

Pearl has had a huge impact on many people, including a little boy named Paxton. He was only seven years old when he asked to see a therapy cat during his stay at the hospital. He had a disease that contorted his hands into something that looked like claws; he couldn't open them. His parents were sitting nearby as Pearl was put down next to him. The family had made the difficult decision to pursue a specific drug to help relax their son's hands, and they were hoping it might work. As Pearl settled in next to Paxton, he began to pet her. Everyone enjoyed the sight of the youngster smiling and petting the cat. And then, slowly over the next ten minutes, his hand opened as he touched Pearl. It was the first time that had occurred, and the family and Paxton were ecstatic. Pearl was part of a miracle that day.

Another incredible story occurred with a teenage girl named Kelsey, who had just been given a terminal diagnosis. She was sobbing, but she wanted to visit with Pearl. Five minutes into the visit, the girl was smiling. When the girl returned to the hospital again, she was at the end of her life. The family specifically requested that Pearl come to visit. Normally, if a patient doesn't interact with Pearl, she only stays for a bit and will come to the side of the bed and put her front paws on Geralyn. That means Pearl is finished. That day Kelsey was completely unresponsive. A family member had to pick up Kelsey's hand to pet Pearl, who sat against her leg the whole time. Pearl never gave any sign she was ready to move on. She was willing to give comfort just by being with Kelsey for as long as she wanted. Pearl seemed to realize that the girl and her family needed this comfort. After a while, Geralyn picked Pearl up and rubbed her paw on Kelsey's arm as a goodbye. Geralyn received an email of appreciation from the staff that was titled: "To say that you and Pearl are amazing would be an understatement."

Helping Nurses

Pearl has become such an important part of the therapy program that her fans include many staff members. One day when she was visiting, two staff members came running over to Pearl and intercepted her as she was about to get on an elevator. They were out of breath, and they exclaimed, "we heard Pearl was in the hospital and we ran over from the other wing because we wanted to see her!"

Perhaps that's why Pearl has been asked to provide therapy to the staff. During one tough month, there were several deaths in the pediatric ward, which deeply upset the staff. Pearl was asked to come over and provide some relief. Geralyn watched as her cat sat on several nurses' laps. Some of them began to cry as they pet the cat. The nurses were overwhelmed with emotion and were so thankful to have an animal to comfort them. That month, Pearl made it onto the *Wall of Thanks*, the university newsletter that recognizes people, and now animals, who have made a difference to the hospital.

Unusual Sensitivity

Geralyn regards her bond with Pearl as one of the most important relationships of her life. Pearl is so sensitive to her caretaker that when Geralyn had a concussion and vertigo, Pearl wouldn't leave her side. Geralyn was on her back for several days, and Pearl seemed to feel it was her duty to take care of her. Apparently, this duty extended to showering, because Pearl went with Geralyn to the bathroom and stood outside the shower while she bathed.

When Geralyn had to euthanize her beloved dog, Pearl was there when she returned from the vet, and she spent the night cuddling Geralyn and her husband. Pearl doesn't usually sleep with them, but she seemed to understand that they needed her comfort that night. Pearl is most definitely a cat who will make you question your stereotypes about felines.

Pearl (Photo courtesy of Geralyn Hawk)

Chapter 4: Lola, A Dumpster Cat, Creates A Writer

Little did Dawn White know, back in 2011 when she was on Facebook looking for a cat sitter, that it would bring her not just a new feline friend but a new career. While browsing, her attention was captured by the forlorn picture of a tabby kitten named Lola. The poor creature had been found in a dumpster, abandoned and ill. She was taken to New York City Animal Care and Control (NYACC) and then pulled out by Leslie Kaufman, owner of On All Fours Cat Sitting, because she was close to being euthanized. Something about Lola's picture captivated Dawn, and she messaged Leslie to see if she could meet the stray kitten.

Dawn had a cat at home named Lexy who seemed lonely, and she thought that Lola might be good company for her. Dawn went to Manhattan Cat Specialists in Manhattan to meet Lola, who was skinny, snotty, and clearly sick. She wasn't going to win any beauty contests. Some people might have looked at Lola, realized there would be high vet bills ahead, and taken a pass. But not Dawn. She had an instant reaction to the kitten and felt a bond with the creature. She decided to adopt her.

Leslie had been posting Lola's story on Facebook, so the kitten already had a following when Dawn met her. Dawn learned that many people still wanted regular updates about the kitten after she was adopted. So Dawn created a Facebook page called "Lola the Rescued Cat," where she continued Lola's story in the kitten's voice. Its initial following grew to nearly 10,000 people as of December 2022.

Lola's story began with finding herself in a dumpster, getting adopted by Dawn, and being brought to her "forever home." Her first few days at Dawn's house, including her initial meeting with Lexy, didn't go well, but over time the two cats worked out their issues. Lola was sick in her early life with Dawn, but numerous trips to the vet and several medications later, she started to thrive. Her story, told from the kitten's perspective, revealed the vulnerability and suffering that the little creature endured through no fault of her own. Her story also showed her intelligence and emotional connection to those around her.

Dawn continued writing about Lola, posting updates on Facebook to show Lola's journey from dumpster to a loving home. Her goal was to educate people about the value of rescue animals. As she explained, "if I could help at least one other animal and change how people view stray cats, it would be worth it to me." During the time she shared Lola's story, she also used Facebook to create auctions for needy animals, raising an impressive $30,000–$40,000 for several rescue groups, as well as individuals with high vet bills.

Dawn believes that Lola led her to become an advocate for cats. Before meeting Lola, she didn't know anything about rescuing stray cats or about Trap-Neuter-Return (TNR) programs for feral cats. As a result of her writing, she's interacted with a larger rescue community and learned about the plight of these felines. And the more she's learned, the more she's realized her writing makes a difference. In 2014, she turned Lola's story into a book, *Lola: Diary of a Rescued Cat*[iii]. She donates ten percent of the book's earnings to animal rescue organizations who help cats in need.

Writing and More Writing

Lola also inspired Dawn to create a blog[iv] where she reviews products, gives advice, and educates the cat community about animal advocacy, rescue, and health and safety issues. She's traveled to cat cafes in Houston, St. Louis, Florida, New York City, and Nashville, sharing reports about them with her readers. She's also part of the Jackson Galaxy Project's Cat Pawsitive Program as a contributing writer. The program is a positive-reinforcement clicker training initiative that enriches day-to-day life for cats in shelters, builds new skills for cats, helps shelter staff/volunteers, promotes the human-cat bond, and helps improve cat adoptability. And she's volunteered for Jackson Galaxy's table at Cat Camp NYC to bring attention to the program and to Jackson's work.

Dawn's writing also led her to become a part of the Cat Writer's Association (CWA), a professional organization dedicated to advancing a wide variety of writing about cats in journalism, social media, radio, television, podcasts, websites, and blogs. Her writing has received fifteen different awards of excellence from the CWA. And in 2018, she was awarded the organization's coveted Muse Medallion for Best Rescue Advocacy Blog. Dawn is clearly being recognized for the impact she's having.

She explained how writing has changed her life. "Writing really enhances my life and makes me happy. With my writing I can open people's eyes. People can see through my work and through Lola's life and realize that those 'damaged' cats are sometimes the best pets you can have."

Adopting Lola and advocating for stray cats has also changed Dawn a great deal as a person. She's more outgoing than she used to be, and she networks, talks, and pitches her book and blog to major brands and cat enthusiasts. She interacts with other bloggers and visits their pages, creating connections in the animal community. It's brought her out of her shell. She used to be shy and described herself as a wallflower. But not anymore.

Dawn is also aware that she's learned about the importance of character from her cat. "Lola has taught me that with love, you can overcome anything, and that forgiveness is very powerful. Lola was obviously someone's cat who was thrown away. And yet, Lola doesn't hold grudges and she loves people. She was fearful in the beginning and used to hide because she was afraid. But she's happy now, and she lives her life in the moment."

In addition to holding a full-time job as an associate vice president of a large nonprofit that provides services to adults with intellectual disabilities, Dawn spends about twenty hours a week on her passion. She's exceedingly busy, but she's found a place to advocate, educate, and make a difference for cats. And it all started with a little tabby who was thrown into a dumpster.

Lola (Photo courtesy of Dawn White)

Chapter 5: Rascal, The Cat Who Consoled and Gave Courage for A New Life

Some cats can enrich an already thriving life whereas others can help a person return from unbearable depths. Leanna Hall was not born to privilege and struggled as a teenager. She found herself homeless when her mother kicked her out of the house during her senior year of high school. Her mother didn't approve of her boyfriend, so she gave her daughter an ultimatum: either break up or move out. Leanna was in love, so she left her home without a place to live. Her boyfriend, Jim, suggested she move in with him and his parents. Leanna had only been dating him for a few months, but she had nowhere else to go, so she agreed.

Abusive Boyfriend

Jim seemed so wonderful when he and Leanna first started dating. He brought her little gifts and seemed to care so much about her. But Leanna's mother was right: Jim wasn't a great guy. Over time, he became possessive and eventually became psychologically abusive. Routine interactions between Jim and Leanna quickly escalated into horrendous fights. At her high school graduation, she briefly spoke with a man next to her, and Jim berated her for being flirtatious. The ceremony was already difficult because none of Leanna's family showed up, so to have her boyfriend severely criticize her for something she didn't do greatly upset her. She ended up crying so much his parents noticed. Jim lied to them and said that she was crying tears of joy.

But joy wasn't something Leanna experienced often during that time. She became anxious and nervous when she interacted with men because of Jim's jealousy. It seemed that anytime she even talked with another man, Jim became furious. One time she was stopped by the police for expired license plates. After conversing with the officer, the couple drove off and Jim accused her of flirting with the man. Jim often later regretted his behavior, and they would make up. Leanna felt like she was on a rollercoaster and hoped that things would improve over time.

After living with his parents for a few months, Jim and Leanna moved out and got a place together. And that's when he gave her a gift that would change her life: a cat named Rascal. The kitten had a grey body with white paws, and he bonded with Leanna immediately. Rascal was the most positive part of her life with Jim during this time. Their relationship continued to deteriorate, and they fought constantly. As she began to question whether she should stay with Jim, Leanna realized she was pregnant. She was young and unsure of her future. She had never thought about having children, but she didn't want to have an abortion. She wanted to give this little human being a life, but she also felt she was too young to care for a child. While Leanna debated what to do, her body made the decision for her; she began having symptoms of a miscarriage: bleeding, cramping, and back pain. She went to the hospital, where she lost the child.

Grief from a Miscarriage

Leanna was overwhelmed with grief. When she turned to Jim for comfort, he blamed her for it. "You should have been more careful!" he screamed at her. Blindsided by his anger, she went to her bedroom. It was there that Rascal offered her the comfort she couldn't find anywhere else. He curled up next to her on her bed and lay exactly where the baby had been.

The miscarriage left Leanna devastated and distraught. She cried every day, lost weight, and felt hopeless about life. The only creature who made her feel better was Rascal; she would pet him for hours. At night he would lie next to her and comfort her. Leanna feels she might not have made it through this trauma of her life if it hadn't been for Rascal.

Independent Life

Eventually Leanna recovered enough to leave her abusive boyfriend. She took Rascal and started a new life. Now when she feels anxious, sad, or upset, Rascal senses her moods and comes to her. She calls him her "emotional support animal" and he's helped her through her emotional hell. The connection they have is deep, as Leanna explained.

> *"I really don't know where I would be if I didn't have him. We have such connection and attachment to each other that I can't even describe it with words. I think it's similar to what my friends have with their kids. I actually carry him like a baby, like you would if you were burping a child; he puts his head on my shoulder. When I've been gone all day, he won't stop following me around until I pick him up and put him on my shoulder. I know Rascal's every meow: when he is hungry, bored, wants to play, and wants attention. He is very talkative and always has something to say. All my friends know how much I love my cat, but nobody really understands our connection."*

Leanna became a student, majoring in business at a local college. She hopes to open a Cat Café after graduation to show others how much these creatures can help us during times of turmoil.

Leanna and Rascal
(Photo courtesy of Leanna Hall)

Chapter 6: Peach, Pushing the Boundaries of What We Believe Cats Can Do

I'm sure few people believe cats can be trained just like dogs. Tori Peterson, a spunky, dark-haired woman who has a lot of energy when she talks, used to be one of these doubters. Tori loves animals, which is not surprising because she's been around them all her life. She grew up on a small farm where she had Nigerian Dwarf goats, rabbits, a mini horse, a pig, and even a yak. Her love for animals led her to study small animal science in Pennsylvania. After she finished her degree, she began working with dogs, both as a behavioral consultant and trainer.

Tori specialized in primitive dogs—breeds that haven't changed much from their ancient ancestors—Central Asian shepherds, Shiba Inus, and Basenjis. These dogs are somewhat catlike in their personalities. They're more fearful and less eager to please than modern breeds and can be challenging to train. Nevertheless, she enjoyed her job and still does dog training and consulting to this day. She didn't think of herself as a cat person and never considered training a cat. Then she met an orange cat she named Peach.

Peach on a Rural Road

Tori had just moved to Wisconsin with her boyfriend, and they were driving around a rural area when they saw something orange run across the road. The couple stopped and Tori went to investigate. She came across a very hungry, weak orange kitten. The little creature had an eye that was swollen and almost completely closed, as well as puncture wounds on her cheek and shoulder. The little kitten didn't run when approached, so Tori picked her up, gave her some dog treats, and took her home. The cat purred incessantly on Tori's lap during the ride. She felt there was something special about this kitten, and even though the couple had just put a deposit on a puppy, they decided to withdraw their money and keep the cat.

Because the kitten seemed to go with the flow and was "just peachy," she earned the name Peach. From the moment she got home, Peach was unusually friendly and wanted to interact with Tori and her boyfriend. She was about twelve weeks old and only weighed about one pound—what healthy kittens weigh at five weeks of age. Tori got her the medical attention she needed and nursed her back to health. She was scheduled to have surgery to stitch up her cheek, but she healed so quickly under Tori's care that she didn't need it. Even in her weakened state, Peach seemed to have a lot of energy and was incessantly curious about her environment and the people around her. She constantly sought attention and would scale curtains, hang upside down off the side of the couch, and look for things and people to engage her.

Cat Training?

Because Peach wanted so much attention (and tended to get into trouble when she was left on her own), Tori began training her. Peach learned basic tricks such as how to sit, and then she advanced to more difficult things. Tori realized Peach liked to learn and enjoyed mastering new tricks—even ones related to feeding time. When it was time to eat, Peach sat on a stool and waited for her food until she was given the command, "Yes! Okay," which meant she could follow Tori out to her cat tree and eat there. Peach learned complex tricks in one to two sessions—much faster than any dogs Tori had trained.

Tori uses the 'Do More With Your Dog!' training program, which has four levels: Novice, Intermediate, Advanced and Expert. Each level requires mastery of a certain set of tricks. A certified person from the training organization looks over each submission and determines if the animal qualifies for that level. Peach quickly progressed to the Expert level. She became one of only three cats who have attained that level. She was so good that she and Tori soon began working on the Championship title. You can see some of her work in videos that have been posted to YouTube. In this first link,[v] Peach is doing the Advanced Trick cat work. You can see her cross her paws, ring a bell, jump up, play the piano, and jump through some hoops. And in this second link,[vi] you see her Expert Trick cat work. She climbs a cage ladder, rolls a peanut, goes shopping, washes her paws, turns off the water, and searches for a specific scent. The last trick is called "nose work," and she's been trained to find birch and cedarwood oil on a very small item, such as a Q-Tip.

Space Cat Academy!

Tori realized Peach wasn't just learning tricks, she was having fun—and the work was creating a strong bond between the two of them. And that gave her an idea: Why not bring this type of training to other cat owners, to improve their bonds with their cats? Perhaps cats who were acting out were just bored and would love to engage with their caretaker and learn something new?

And so, Tori's career changed, and Space Cat Academy was born. She created this business to help cats and caretakers create a stronger connection through education and training. For example, there were courses on how to cut your cat's nails, how to read your cat's body language, how to use a harness, how to reduce furniture scratching, how to get your cat comfortable with a carrier, and many other topics. I bought the course on how to clip your cat's nails and found it useful. Tori also provides consulting services for cat caretakers.[vii]

Peach Teaches Tori

Tori says that Peach has changed her life. She said she never saw the potential to train and change a cat's behaviors or understood how bonded one can be to a feline. Peach taught her about the nature of the cat-human bond and about cats' ability to learn new things. Peach is her best friend, and they understand one another at a deep level. When Tori is stressed or anxious, Peach will press herself against her to comfort her.

And Peach follows her everywhere, including some places she shouldn't. One day when Tori was in the shower, Peach opened the shower door, came inside, and stood there for a few minutes while water sprayed on her. Peach didn't enjoy getting wet and decided to leave. She hopped out of the shower and then closed the door behind her!

Peach is so intelligent she can turn on the living room clapper light on her own, by making a noise. She also opens doors without help and operates her own automatic mouse toys. She started her toy accidentally one time, and now does it on her own when she wants to play.

Peach has been trained to do more than tricks, however. She ventures outdoors on her harness and leash and even goes on road trips across the country to New Jersey a couple times a year. Peach is truly an extraordinary cat who reminds us not to underestimate the felines around us; changing cat behaviors takes time and patience, but it's possible, and cat training can increase the bond between cats and humans.

Peach (Photo courtesy of Tori Peterson)

Peach (Photo courtesy of Tori Peterson)

Chapter 7: Community Cats Create a Fighter

Sometimes living with humans can mean comfort and security for cats, but it can also bring danger and cruelty. Even though she stepped up to advocate for her feline friends, Martha Hernandez said her story wasn't a happy one. It started in 2016 when she moved into an apartment complex in New Jersey. She had never owned a cat and had little affection for them. But when she started living there, she realized the complex had over one hundred feral (cats who are unsocialized to humans) and stray cats roaming around.

The story would have ended there if she hadn't been approached by one of the cats on a summer day, when she was sitting outside with her twelve-year-old daughter. The friendly cat who came over to her was a dark male tabby who liked meeting new people. Martha had seen him strutting around the complex interacting with her neighbors. On that day, he came over to Martha and her daughter and plopped right into their laps. He was a big cat, and he was used to getting a positive reception. It was no different with Martha. Although she wasn't a cat person, she found him charming and named him Tommy. He was visiting another family who considered adopting him, but Martha got to him first and invited Tommy to live with her. He happily became a permanent member of their family.

The next applicant for asylum was a six-month-old kitten. His white fur and big green eyes led Martha to name him Eevee, after a Pokémon character. The little stray came into their lives when he showed up in their courtyard and moved into their home shortly thereafter. A couple months later, the family came upon Dean, a brown and black three-week-old kitten. Dean walked up to

Martha's daughter in the apartment parking lot and cried loudly. They took him to a shelter for an examination, and then Martha began fostering him until he could be adopted. But they grew too attached to Dean and couldn't let him go. They became his forever family shortly thereafter.

Martha couldn't adopt every cat and kitten who was roaming around the complex, so she became involved with 11th Hour Rescue, a volunteer-run animal protection organization in Randolph, New Jersey, that rescues dogs and cats in their "eleventh hour," the time when shelters can no longer care for them, and they're scheduled for euthanasia. The organization often rescues cats and dogs from dire situations and has a network of foster volunteers who provide the animals with love and attention until they find their forever homes. The group also educates the community about the importance of spaying and neutering to reduce the overpopulation of cats and dogs.

Martha would take the kittens to this rescue group, and they would socialize them and then find adopters. Eventually Martha learned about TNR (Trap, Neuter, Return) programs and she would trap, neuter, and then return the adult cats back to the complex. Any kittens would go to 11th Hour Rescue. She learned that returning spayed/neutered stray and feral cats back to their home keeps other cats from moving in and slowly reduces the population (because the cats don't reproduce). It was the safest and most humane way to manage cats who couldn't be adopted.

New Management

All was going well until a new company took over the apartment complex. Within a week, Martha learned that they intended to kill all the cats who had made their home there for many years. Martha and her husband went to the office to discuss the issue. A female manager told them that there was no such plan in place. Martha explained she was a volunteer for 11th Hour Rescue and that she was feeding and caring for several colonies in the complex. The woman reiterated there was no plan to kill the cats.

The next day the entire apartment complex got an email instructing them not to feed any of the cats on the property. Two managers were working with a rescue organization and with the Department of Health to take care of the cats. They also said the cats were carrying infectious agents such as rabies, toxoplasmosis, and other deadly diseases. They viewed the cats as pests. Martha interacted with most cats at the complex and knew they weren't sick. She tried to talk to the management company, but they weren't interested.

Disappearances and Death

One by one, the cats started to disappear. The first victim was a grey cat with white paws whom Martha lovingly nicknamed "Boots." Boots was one of her favorites because he allowed her to pet him, unlike the other feral members of the colony. He was a handsome guy who disappeared for a while and then reappeared looking dreadfully sick: his white paws had turned yellow, and he was drooling uncontrollably and limping. She believed he was poisoned because he showed signs of nerve damage. She never saw him again and cannot speak about him without crying.

Martha learned that the management company was using leg traps—barbaric devices that clamp an animal's leg between spring-loaded jaws—and then spraying the trapped animals with pepper spray. The company also nailed shut the crawl spaces under the homes where many of the cats lived. One of the workers admitted to Martha they had been told to kill every cat on the premises, using any means possible. The management was vicious in their determination to exterminate the cats. The level of animal cruelty was unimaginable. Martha became frantic trying to save them all.

She opened the crawl spaces they nailed shut. She complained publicly to the management company and created a Facebook page[viii] about what was happening in her community. The images from her posts were graphic and disturbing, so that they would create outrage and motivate action. Martha also started catching the cats and taking them to the veterinarian, creating a GoFundMe for cats who were injured or poisoned. One poor kitten named Frankie was caught in a cruel leg trap, and she raised money to amputate his leg. Sadly, Frankie didn't survive the surgery.

Harassment

The management company responded to Martha's efforts by putting dead cats in front of her home. They tried to evict her by closing the payment portal she used and then claimed she wasn't paying her rent. Then they took away her parking space and added bogus charges to her monthly bill to pressure her to leave. The harassment was constant. Martha would not be intimidated, and she continued to fight for her sweet creatures.

But the cats continued to die. One of her favorite orange tabby cats, Malone, passed away right in front of her, while another cat, Sweet Pete, died in her arms. Her colony of thirty cats dwindled to ten. Martha was distraught with grief. She couldn't believe how cruel these people were or understand why the cats were being treated so terribly.

Martha continued to fight for the cats even after she got evicted from the complex. She devoted herself to caring for the cats who were left behind. She eventually trapped most of them and relocated them to an area where they wouldn't be in danger.

I asked Martha how she had changed as a result of this experience and her answer was immediate, "I'm a kinder person and I take care of the creatures around me. And I'm also stronger. Those cats gave me the strength to fight. I had no idea how bold I could be or where that strength came from. But I knew I had to stand up and be a voice for those who were suffering. And I'm still talking, I'm still taking care of them, and I'm not turning my back."

When I asked her about the cats who are gone, she simply replied, "they didn't die for no reason. I'll fight for them, and I'll love them for the rest of my life."

Community cats in New Jersey created a fighter. Keep fighting, Martha!

Boots, a community cat
(Photo courtesy of Martha Hernandez)

Chapter 8: Belle, Healing Attendant

Although people are generally the ones who rescue cats, sometimes they return the favor. Timothy Moncivaiz speaks of his cat, Belle, with a certain reverence for that reason. Belle is a greyish-brown tabby who began her life in Costa Rica. She's lucky to be alive because she was abandoned in a sewer as a kitten. She was rescued by Tim's fiancée, Crystal, when she and Tim lived in Costa Rica as students. When they relocated back to the United States, Belle came along too.

Tim described eight-year-old Belle as having the personality of an older lady who likes everything her way. Belle wasn't thrilled when the couple adopted a small dog named Lucy, but she eventually accepted Lucy into the family. Belle's fussy personality doesn't bother Tim in the least, however, because she played an important role during a scary time when he had a staph infection.

Infection

It all started when Tim experienced pain in his leg. He assumed it was a sprained ankle and wore a brace to stabilize it. He wore the support for several days and developed a blister. When the blister burst, it offered a pathway for a staph infection to develop. *Staphylococcus* bacteria are commonly found on the skin and are usually benign. However, in Tim's case the staph was aggressive because it was caused by a diabetic ulcer, not a sprained ankle.

The infection was exceptionally painful for Tim, and three weeks before Christmas he was laid up on his couch. Between the pain and the painkillers, he was unable to do anything for himself. He needed help eating, getting up, going to the restroom, and dressing.

While Tim rested on the couch, Belle and his dog, Lucy, were by his side night and day. Belle lay next to his leg and Lucy lay behind his head. Both animals were highly vigilant toward their patient, watching him closely. Belle would spend most of her time curled next to Tim's injured leg, purring as much as she could.

Hospital Stay and Surgery

On December twenty-third, Tim was admitted to the hospital for the infection, which had gotten worse. And on Christmas Eve, a surgeon came to his bed and told him the flesh on his leg was dead, and that surgery would be required to completely remove the infection. He explained there was an eighty-five percent chance the leg would have to be amputated. Tim was terrified.

During his stay at the hospital, Crystal noticed the animals were agitated. Both Belle and Lucy walked around the house, looking into every room. Belle often made long crying sounds and Lucy whined. They seemed worried that something had happened to Tim. And their agitation increased as Crystal and Tim's mother spent more time at the hospital than at home.

The surgery was successful, and luckily Tim didn't lose his leg. After leaving the hospital, he was back on the couch, where he lay for the next three months. He was in tremendous pain, unable to use the affected leg, but Belle and Lucy were happy to have him home. However, because he was unable to walk, and because Crystal had to leave home for work, they decided to have Lucy stay with his mom during his recovery. From that point on, it was just Belle and Tim.

Recovery

Belle took her job as chief animal healer seriously. She stayed by Tim's side and purred next to his wound. Tim believes she was trying to heal him, because cats often do that when they're in pain. Studies suggest that purring stimulates cats' healing, so perhaps she was responding to his pain. He thinks her purring may have actually stimulated his own healing. Or perhaps having her always at his side made him feel cared for and secure, which helped his recovery.

Three months later, Tim could only do a few things. He was able to move around a little with the use of a walker, a crutch, or a cane and get his weekly antibiotics, which were administered intravenously. But he often was exhausted and lay on the couch. It was a difficult time, but Belle was always there, and she encouraged him to get up and feed her, which offered him a little physical therapy. And when he was too weak to move, she would lie by his side. Eventually Tim was able to go to work. The day he left the house, Belle made a mournful cry, which Crystal thought was an attempt to get Tim to come back.

Belle showed tremendous patience in caring for Tim, even though she was the only animal in the house. Crystal and Tim thought she might be lonely, so they adopted a kitten named Olive, who seemed to take cues from Belle in caring for Tim. Olive apparently felt she was in charge of Tim's sleeping schedule and began making a racket if he didn't go to bed at the appointed hour. Meanwhile, Belle maintained her caring regimen and curled up next to him whenever possible. Tim believes that without his animal's care he wouldn't be where he is today. And Tim and Crystal both believe that Belle's nursing him was a way of returning the favor of being rescued all those years ago.

Belle
(Photo courtesy of Timothy Moncivaiz)

Chapter 9: Tommy, Educating Us About Special Needs

Tommy is an eight-year-old grayish-brown tabby cat who has prevailed against the odds, not only to survive, but to thrive and spread joy to those he meets. He was found in a terrible hoarding situation and then dumped at a local veterinarian's office. That's where Christy Santoro found him when he was only a few weeks old. Tommy's eyes were completely closed, and when they opened, it was obvious they were infected. The veterinarian tried to save his eyes, but it was impossible. He had to have both eyes removed. But Tommy's blindness has had no impact on his personality. He wants to interact with lots of people and he's a good-natured, mellow cat. Christy says she's never heard him hiss or growl—not even once.

Tommy loves being outside, loves going places, and particularly enjoys being wheeled around in his cat stroller. Because he is so imperturbable, Christy got him certified as a therapy animal through Pet Partners. He passed his test with flying colors. Christy claims the two of them have a very special bond—he follows her everywhere and sleeps next to her at night. And no matter whom he visits, he always gives unconditional positive regard, which is why so many people like him.

Tommy, the Fundraiser (and Big Kisser)

Tommy is apparently a great addition to any fundraiser because he's so easygoing. Christy installed Tommy in a Kissing Booth for a cat café fundraiser. Tommy is apparently quite the lover. People came up to him for two hours and gave money just to receive a peck from Tommy. Apparently, his presence (and smooching) led to some big donations. That day, he made over $500 for the cat café. He's also done kissing booths at several nonprofit animal rescues in Las Vegas.

Tommy Visits Schools and Special-Care Facilities

Tommy loves people so much that Christy can bring him to schools, where he interacts with children of all ages. He visits kids in elementary, junior high, and high schools. Children always ask about his blindness and whether it affects him. Through his presence, he shows the children that having special needs and being different isn't bad. He's particularly popular with kids from special-education classes, who can relate to the fact he's not like other cats.

Because he's so great with people, Tommy has become part of a therapy program at an assisted-living facility. One woman he regularly visits has lost the ability to walk, so Tommy lies next to her on her bed while she pets him. They have a lovely connection. Sometimes he sits right on her chest and purrs away. She always looks forward to Tommy's visits and says it's one of the best parts of her week.

Tommy also visits a memory-care center, where the residents battle dementia and Alzheimer's disease. He's made a big difference with some of these folks. One woman that Tommy met became very agitated and confused. She was yelling for her husband, saying she wanted to go home, wanted her car keys, and would not stay. Unfortunately, her husband had passed away and she no longer lived in the home she thought she inhabited. Tommy climbed into her lap, and within a few seconds, she relaxed. Before long, she stopped focusing on wanting to leave and started talking about her own cat.

State Employees in High-Stress Positions

Tommy also helps people who have high-stress jobs, like those who work for the county and who manage elder-abuse and child-welfare cases. These jobs take their toll on these employees. Occasionally, the county hosts a wellness event for these workers. They often have therapy dogs there too, but Tommy is a great favorite and many of the attendees wait in line to pet him and get his kindness and comfort.

Helping Victims of the Las Vegas Mass Shooting

Another group Tommy has helped are the victims of the Las Vegas mass shooting that occurred on October 1, 2017. On that night, a man opened fire on a crowd of concertgoers at the Route 91 Harvest music festival. He killed fifty-eight people and wounded 413. Because people started running in panic, the injury total rose to 869. The incident became the largest mass shooting in the United States to date. The Las Vegas Resiliency Center has an annual event where they invite victims of this tragedy to find comfort. They have evening massages, yoga, and sessions with therapy animals. Christy has seen Tommy sit on victims' laps as they cry and tell him what it was like to experience this horrific event. Tommy seems able to ease their grief and make them feel better.

Tommy Cat Foundation

Christy feels so strongly about the work that she and Tommy do, she's created the Tommy Cat Foundation. Their website explains, "I'm a very special guy that's blind. I want to bring attention to the greatness of pets with special needs and help others in need." The Tommy Cat Foundation rescues and cares for special-needs cats, providing a loving home and coverage of all medical care. It's a 501(c)(3) nonprofit organization.

If you ever get to interact with Tommy, you'll no doubt agree that he's truly special. Although he doesn't have eyes, he sees more than most, and he is a loving, calming influence for those in need.

Tommy (Photo courtesy of Christy Santoro)

Chapter 10: Zack, Socializer & Calming Influence for an Anxious Teenager

If you ever meet Chris Wall, you'll see an attractive, energetic young woman with long brown hair and trendy glasses who speaks clearly and concisely. She seems to have the world at her feet as she tells you about her plans to go to college. You'd never guess that she's fought her share of demons and that a little cat named Zack is part of the reason she's able to face the world. Zack helped her combat her anxiety, assisted her in making friends, and taught her some major life lessons.

Chris' problems started when she was young; she was home-schooled for the first few years. When she was in fourth grade, her parents decided to send her to a private school. And that's when her anxiety started. The combination of leaving her home, some pre-existing family issues, and her lack of exposure to kids her age sent her into a tailspin. She always felt apprehensive when she arrived at school. Unfortunately, other students perceived her as a weird kid because she didn't know how to interact with those her own age. And her inability to socialize with other children created even more anxiety. She recalled feeling lonely at school. One day at recess, she decided to chase a squirrel because she didn't know what else to do.

Zack and the Janitor's Closet

Chris' difficulties continued unabated until sixth grade, which is when Zack, a white and orange tabby cat, came into her life. He was just a kitten when he was found in a janitor's closet by neighbors who lived down the street. They brought the kitten home but the other cat in the household didn't like him and hissed continually at Zack. The family decided the kitten needed a different home.

Chris and a friend went to see the kitten. Zack wanted nothing to do with her friend, but when he saw Chris, he perked up and walked right over to her. Within seconds, he crawled into her arms. It's as if he already knew her. She decided to adopt Zack and took him home, installing him in her bedroom. Luckily her parents agreed with her plan after she told them how much she liked the kitten. Zack and Chris were inseparable from that moment forward.

Zack helps her a great deal and is a calming influence. Because Chris sleeps in a bedroom in the basement, it's very dark and she often awakes with anxiety during the night. Zack is so sensitive to her issues that he comes to her during an anxiety attack and presses his body against her. It calms her tremendously and allows her to get back to sleep. She notices that on nights when she's particularly upset, he sleeps right next to her and won't leave her side.

Zack Helps Chris Socialize

Zack also helped his companion socialize with other kids her age. If a potential friend came to the house, Chris would ask if the child wanted to meet her cat. The answer was always "yes," and they would go and pet Zack, which would lead to an easy conversation about her cat. Zack went along with these petting/socializing sessions and would follow Chris and the friend around her home, thus becoming the focal point for the visit. Suddenly interacting with other kids wasn't so difficult. Zack helped her make that transition from "weird kid" to the vivacious person she is now.

Zack Needs Help

Zack also taught Chris about taking care of others—specifically him. It all started when the family tried having a dog in the home. Everything was going well until a loud bang startled the dog, who immediately attacked Zack. He grabbed the cat's head in his mouth. Chris still shudders when she talks about it, for Zack's head was almost entirely inside the dog's mouth, his body was dangling outside, and his claws were on the dog's mouth. Both animals were frozen. The family managed to pry open the dog's mouth with a stick and remove the poor cat, whose jaw and tongue were permanently damaged. That night in the veterinary emergency room, Chris was inconsolable as she prayed her cat would survive. She couldn't imagine life without him.

Zack was seriously emotionally and physically scarred by the dog attack, and he developed the same anxiety that plagued Chris. She began comforting and taking care of him. He followed her around, needing to always be near her. She understood his affliction because she suffered from the same thing. When he started to panic, she would pick him up and hold him tightly. He also had seizures, which Chris managed by holding him carefully and rubbing his face. Over time, he's become less anxious because of her ministrations. Interestingly, both take medication to manage their anxiety.

A Lasting Influence

When Chris talks about Zack, you can see how much she loves him and how thankful she is to have him in her life. He comforted her during some of her toughest hours and helped her socialize with other kids. And he also taught her how to care for another creature and how much of a difference she can make in others' lives. When someone says something disparaging about cats, she gets upset because she's seen so much goodness in a little cat named Zack. She will forever be changed because of him, for he's helped her become the lovely woman she is today.

Zack (Photo courtesy of Chris Wall)

Chapter 11: Community Cats Bring People Together

Patty Reynolds lives in Moravia, a village of 1,200 people in upstate New York. She lived there for twenty years when she retired from her job at nearby Cornell University. She served as a licensed veterinary technician for thirty-six years and began looking for something meaningful to fill her time. Who knew that she would find it in an unlikely place, with an animal she thought she disliked?

It all started when Patty's friend, Gail Morse had a handyman who mentioned there were a lot of pregnant stray cats at his trailer park. Gail went with her friend, Gretchen Fickeisen to the trailer park, where they managed the stray-cat situation by spaying the females and finding homes for the kittens. Gail even adopted three of the kittens, who became adored permanent members of the family. After helping the trailer-park residents, Gail and Gretchen decided to take on the feral cats in the village, and Gail posted about the issue on Facebook. Patty saw the post and had been complaining about community cats for twenty years. Even though she had cats in her home, she had no great love for feral cats, because she viewed them as a different cat species.

Still, Patty told Gail she would help her manage the feral-cat problem, and she learned about TNR (Trap-Neuter-Return) programs. She did a Google search that led to Alley Cat Allies, the Kitten Lady, and the Facebook group Trap-Neuter-Return Community.[ix] Within a week, she was trapping cats, holding feral cats in her garage, transporting them to a veterinary clinic to be spayed or neutered, and working to socialize friendly kittens so they could be adopted. She worked closely with Gretchen, who was running a local dog rescue group, the Homestretch Dog Haven, which helped them raise funds for the spaying and neutering of the cats.

Patty quickly realized her backyard had many community cats. She could catch as many as she wanted just by putting traps in her yard. Two cats were even captured on her deck. There was a feral colony about a half block away with great caretakers, but the cats hadn't been altered, so they needed to be trapped and neutered. Patty bought more traps to get this group into the vet. Within two months, her small project turned into a full-time job. And Patty loved it. Suddenly she was passionate about helping cats who would benefit from TNR.

Patty learned that community cats need a community of people. Patty met others who were also trapping feral cats and doing TNR work in the surrounding area. Suddenly, a whole new world opened to her. She made eight new friends, two of whom became extremely close. These women would meet and talk about the cats and how they could deal with certain colonies or manage certain cats who needed to be spayed or neutered. They had a purpose, a shared passion, and they bonded over more than just the cats. They talked about their personal lives, their struggles, and about making a difference.

As she became more involved with the cats, Patty became more connected to the village. Before she discovered TNR, she never felt she was part of the community, even though she lived right in the middle of Moravia. She tried to make stronger relationships but was unable. She didn't have any children—which was how many people bonded—and she couldn't seem to find a way to link up to the people who lived in her area. But now, she's no longer just living in Moravia—she's an integral part of the feral-cat solution and she's more involved with the community than ever before. She has many new friends who live in the village, and she's an essential part of the cat team there.

Over time, Patty has become one of the "experts" whom people consult when they have a feral-cat problem. She's connected with folks in farms surrounding the village, who are taking community cats to live in their barns to control mice and rats. She's often contacted by colony caretakers, who need information or help managing their colonies or who are dealing with cats who have illnesses or injuries.

I asked Patty how the community cats have affected her, and she said, "they've brought me out of my shell. I've always been an introvert, but I've blossomed, and people wouldn't even recognize me now. I'm very comfortable playing the role I play in the village and being the one who helps the cats."

But she's not just helping cats; she's helping people. There are many caretakers who are ashamed to admit that they're tending to community cats. When she recently posted on the Facebook village page for feeders to contact her, only one person responded. They don't like to admit openly that they're feeding because they worry others will harass them. Many cats sleep in people's basements, which can cause property damage and other issues. However, feral cats multiply quickly if they're not managed. An unspayed female can have two to three litters per year, and each litter can have three to five kittens. Even young kittens can reproduce as early as six months of age. One fertile queen cat can lead to twenty-five births in a single year. So by helping the cats and reducing their numbers, she's helping the many feeders avoid situations that are overwhelming.

A small conversation and a little project became a full-time job, a passion, an avenue for meeting others, and a way to make a difference. Community cats have made Patty an important part of her village, and they've brought a group of women together who have made a difference. Patty will always be grateful for these cats and the role they have played in her life.

Gucci, One of Patty's Community Cats
(Photo courtesy of Patty Reynolds)

Chapter 12: Tino, the Intuitive Feline Therapist

Puntino is an adorable black-and-white Devon Rex cat who was born in Italy and goes by the name Tino. He works with a lovely woman named Dannie Sayers in a variety of organizations in Tacoma, Washington, and Indio, California. They live part-time in each of these communities. Ask Dannie to talk about Tino and the stories just tumble out about how he's made a difference in so many people's lives. And according to Dannie, "The longer he does this work, the better he gets."

The Veterans' Feline Therapist

Tino is a regular visitor to one of Washington state's VA Community Living Centers, which provide residential nursing care for disabled veterans. Tino's visits are often the highlight of the week for many of these vets, who suffer from maladies that require a high level of healthcare. A common one is paralysis. But Tino seems to have no issues interacting with people who are unable to move their hands or limbs. One resident's hands were in a frozen position—curving outward, so he couldn't pet the cat as one would normally. Tino knew exactly what to do; he put his head right into the man's hands. The look on the veteran's face was priceless: he broke into a huge smile. Another vet could barely move, and he lay prone in his bed. Tino again knew what to do; he got onto the man's bed and snuggled under his chin. The man loved it and always relaxed when Tino visited. Yet another fan of Tino's was a man who was paralyzed and unable to talk; he just moaned. When Dannie placed

Tino on the man's belly, the cat snuggled into his hands. The man stopped moaning and relaxed. It was pure joy.

Even the veterans who don't want to pet Tino appreciate his visits. One man was sharing a room with someone whom Tino visited regularly. When Dannie made her rounds, she talked with the roommate while Tino sat patiently in his stroller and interacted with the man who requested his company. This situation went on for six months. And although the veteran didn't want to interact with Tino, he always let the nurses know he wanted Dannie and Tino to stop by. Finally, Dannie stopped by with Tino to talk, and the cat indicated he wanted to sit in the man's lap. Dannie wasn't sure if it was a good idea, so she asked if it was okay. The answer was a definite yes. Somehow Tino knew exactly when the vet wanted to hold him. It was a special moment for both Dannie and Tino.

One of the vets' favorite activities is to go fishing at a nearby lake. One day when Tino came to visit, many of the residents were away at the lake, so Dannie brought the cat out to see them. Tino sat next to several residents while they fished. Dannie captured a picture of one veteran who had one hand on Tino and the other hand on his fishing pole. It was a touching moment for both Tino and the vets, who enjoyed the day a great deal.

Tino at the lake
(Photo courtesy of Danny Sayers)

Memory Care and Managing Families

Tino also works in a memory-care unit, where he navigates complex emotional situations. In one unit, a man suffered from depression. He liked Tino, but when he got depressed, he didn't want any company. One day they went to see him. Just as he started to say he didn't want a visitor, Tino got onto his bed and put his head right under the man's armpit. Tino kept bumping him until he engaged with the cat. The man was glad afterward and thanked them for visiting. "You make me feel a whole lot better, Tino," he said as they left.

Many people have a difficult time placing their family members into these units. One of the nurses asked Dannie if she could bring Tino to visit a woman with dementia who was being admitted. She'd lost all semblance of communication and was holding a doll. She wasn't responsive to anyone, including her spouse of many years. Tino initially went over to her, but then realized where he was really needed. He hopped onto her husband's lap and comforted him as he said goodbye to his wife. The man sat and petted Tino as he got used to the idea that he was going home without his beloved partner.

In another situation, the staff asked Dannie if Tino would help a new resident while his family was trying to leave. In this case, an older man was being admitted. Tino ended up interacting with the whole family during that visit, which gave them something to focus on other than their pain. Tino finally went to snuggle with the man, which made it easier for the family to leave. They walked out, leaving their relative sitting in his wheelchair with Tino on his lap.

Talk Therapy (with a Cat)

Wherever Tino goes, he's made a difference. Dannie recounted one story of a ninety-three-year-old lady who lived in a rehab and health care facility in Palm Springs. Tino would lie on the bed next to her while she shared her life story. Dannie learned that she was living in England during World War II when she met an American soldier and fell in love. They were intimate once before he left for France to fight. Unfortunately, he was killed in battle, and she realized she was pregnant soon afterward. Eventually she emigrated to the United States with the help of an immigration attorney. Her son was three years old when she arrived in America. The lovely part of the story was that she ended up marrying her good Samaritan immigration attorney and had three children with him. She revealed many things about her life because of the calm, trusting relationship that Tino and Dannie created with her.

Hard Work, Much Communication

Dannie continues to be impressed with her cat and the work he does. She's learned that he understands whom to engage, how to interact with them, and when to leave. She and Tino communicate a great deal during their visits. She looks to him to get her cues and knows not to rush him. When he wants to leave, he looks at her and signals that it's time to go. He just knows. It's hard work. As a result, he's very tired after these visits and will sleep soundly.

It's not surprising that Tino and Dannie are applying for the new Animal-Assisted Crisis Response (AACR) group through Pet Partners. They will get certified after taking additional training about responding to crisis situations. They will be helping so many people who truly need it. Thank you, Tino.

Tino—just arrived and ready for work
(Photo Courtesy of Danny Sayers)

Chapter 13: July, Simply an Angel

Some felines have an uncanny, almost supernatural talent for sharing love with their companions. No one needed this help more than a woman named Lori. Every July 25, she was inconsolable. The day would creep up on her and hit her with incredible force. The memories of her daughter would flood in and overwhelm her; she would be unable to do anything except cry. The pain occurred for several years—ever since Lori had lost her daughter, Ashley Rae.

Ashley Rae was a bright, talented seventeen-year-old girl who was incredibly sensitive. She was an animal person—she couldn't bear to see an animal hurt in any way. Once she and her boyfriend accidentally hit a baby fox when they were driving. They pulled over to see if they could help it, but it was dead. Ashley said a prayer for the fox and then cried for days. If there was a person who embodied true kindness and sensitivity, it was Ashley.

Ashley was driving home from seeing her boyfriend on July 25 when she skidded off the road and hit a tree. The tire tracks suggested she swerved to avoid hitting something—perhaps an animal. No one will ever know what happened except Ashley. The days and weeks that followed her passing were the most impossible ones for her mother. Lori couldn't make sense of the tragedy. Why had this happened? Why had it happened to her daughter—a bright, beautiful, and kind person? How could God have taken someone like Ashley, who had so much promise?

The grief overwhelmed Lori, who had trouble working, sleeping, and living until one day in 2016. Lori was driving home when she saw a kitten scamper under a parked van where two little boys were standing. The boys tried to retrieve the kitten. When she came out of her vehicle a few moments later, she saw the two boys heading down the road holding the kitten.

"Is this your kitten?" she asked.

"No."

"Do you know who it belongs to?"

They both shook their heads no.

Lori reached out and pet the kitten, who responded affectionately.

"The kitten seems really friendly," she said.

"Yeah, it's really, really friendly," one of the boys said with a big smile.

"What are you doing with the cat?" she asked.

"We're playing with it."

"And what are you planning on doing with the cat once you're done playing?" Lori said with concern.

"Let it go," one boy said.

"Can I have the cat?" Lori asked. She didn't know why, but she felt compelled to rescue the stray.

The boys gave her the kitten and she took it inside. The creature was emaciated, had a broken tail, and was dirty. It was about six months old, but only weighed four pounds. It appeared to be a mixture of a shorthair tabby and a Maine Coon cat, with a fluffy tail and brown ear tufts. She gave the kitten a flea bath, then called around to see if any local shelter would be interested in putting it on their adoption floor.

She found a shelter and started to prepare the kitten for its adoption. Lori wanted to feed the kitten for a few days, so it gained weight, and she wanted to get a sense of its temperament. However, during the next few days, Lori felt that something about this animal was different. When Lori interacted with the kitten, she seemed to respond to her in a way that cats don't normally react. For one thing, she would play fetch with Lori. And then there was the way the cat seemed to look at Lori, as if she understood her pain.

Lori became attached and decided to keep her. She named her July (pronounced JOOL-ee). July waited for her and greeted her every day when she came home from work. And when Lori was bereft, the cat climbed into her lap. July was the antidepressant Lori so badly needed. One day, when Lori was missing her daughter and crying, July climbed into her lap and comforted her. Lori looked down at July and said: "Why are you here?"

July looked at her steadfastly and never broke her gaze. Most cats stare when they're trying to be aggressive, but July used her eyes to communicate that she cared. It was almost as if she was answering Lori's question by asking, "Don't you know why I'm here?"

After a couple of weeks and a visit to the veterinarian, Lori introduced July to the other cats in the household, and something unusual happened. All the cats immediately accepted July as if she'd lived there for years. The first few times they interacted with her they didn't hiss or become upset, which usually happened when they were faced with a new cat. In fact, July jumped into a cat tree with all the other cats, as if they had always lived together.

Lori felt the cat was uniquely sensitive to her in a way she hadn't experienced from an animal. And July reminded her of her daughter, who had a similar sensitivity, kindness, and demeanor.

Lori was skeptical but felt divine intervention explained July's presence in her life. She believed that if her daughter could have sent her a gift from beyond the grave, July was that gift. She thinks the cat was put into her life as a way for her to focus less on her grief and more on the living people and animals who surrounded her.

July's presence was tremendously therapeutic for Lori. The cat gave Lori a place to put her grief, a creature who could comfort her, and a feeling that life could go on without her daughter. We'll never know what forces lie behind the major things that happen to us, but July was the cat who finally moved Lori from her unspeakable grief into a place where she could love and focus on another being.

Chapter 14: Basil, A Calming Influence Wherever She Goes

Tina Parkhurst's cat, Basil, had a rough early life. She was found in a field, starving and close to death. Tina saved Basil by bottle-feeding her. Basil's early life and her bond with Tina may be some of the reasons she's special. But Basil is rare to begin with: she's an orange tuxedo cat, which is unusual because only fifteen to twenty percent of orange tabbies are female. She's also one of only 222 cats who are certified through Pet Partners. Even more important, she's certified for complex, unpredictable environments, which means that she's the crème de la crème of feline therapists. And she loves the work. Even after years of working as a therapy animal, when Tina jingles her harness, she comes running.

Hospital Therapist

Few hospitals allow therapy cats because many administrators mistakenly believe cats carry contagious diseases and can't be trained. Both myths are untrue. The most progressive facilities, such as Oregon Health Science University Hospital, have realized that cats are highly effective therapy animals. But therapy cats are not as common as therapy dogs. Out of the twenty-one animal service teams the hospital employs, Basil is only one of two cat teams. Tina adheres to special requirements to provide therapy at the hospital. She bathes Basil twenty-four hours before each visit and puts sheets or blankets in between Basil and the patients' beds. But it's all worth it; there are currently more requests for cat therapy visits than dog ones.

Interestingly, all Pet Partners therapy cat teams are held to the same standards for training, hygiene, and behavior as the dog teams. And while cat teams go through the same evaluation process as the dog teams, their requirements are tougher: cats are checked for their reactions to dogs during an evaluation, but dogs aren't evaluated for their responses to any other species. Tina has discovered that although therapy cats are held to a higher standard, they're seldom given the recognition or respect they deserve for the work they do.

Basil is the Needed Ingredient

One day, Tina was with Basil at a farmer's market when a woman approached and said, "my mother is at a care facility up the road, and I'm wondering if you would visit her. Could you do that?" The woman's mother, Eva, had dementia and it was getting worse. Dementia patients sometimes become aggressive and are easily upset. Eva was so agitated she wasn't sleeping. Tina and Basil went to visit her. The elderly woman sat in a recliner with swollen legs. Basil sat on her lap and snuggled her. Within five minutes both she and Basil were sleeping. The daughter was so amazed she cried. She thanked Tina profusely and explained, "my mother hasn't slept for days!" Tina and Basil stayed for forty-five minutes, and when they left, Eva was still sleeping soundly.

Another notable patient whom Basil and Tina visited was Valerie, a woman in her nineties. They called on her many times, and she shared her life story with them. She was a war bride from Australia, and she told Tina wonderful anecdotes about what Australia and Sydney were like before World War II. They visited her in several different facilities, as she transitioned from a rehabilitation center to an elder-care home. She always enjoyed seeing Basil and would greet the cat saying, "Hello, love!" The last time they saw her, she was at the end of her life, on morphine and unable to talk. Tina put Basil next to her and then, to everyone's shock, Valerie smiled slightly. She couldn't speak, but she let them know how much she appreciated their visit.

"I only want one thing…"

On one of the therapy team's regular visits to the physical rehabilitation center, some nurses approached Tina and asked if she and Basil would visit with a special patient. They readily agreed to meet Sly, short for Sylvester, an elderly man who had just been given a terminal cancer diagnosis; he had two months to live. When the staff learned his prognosis, they told him he could have whatever he wanted. If he wanted ice cream three times a day, that was fine with them. Sly responded, "I only want one thing…to have a cat on my lap." And that's when Basil and Tina started to visit him. For about six weeks, they visited Sly as he told them stories of how he grew up in St. Louis and what his early life was like. Basil would sit in his lap while he stroked her. The last week they visited, he was dying. Sly said nothing, but Basil sat on his lap, and he touched the cat. He passed away that night, having received the one thing he wanted most: Basil, who comforted him on his last day.

Cats Comfort

Given Basil's abilities, Tina registered them as an Animal-Assisted Crisis Response Team through Pet Partners. These teams are available in the United States in case of a crisis, such as a shooting or natural emergency. Qualified teams work with agencies to offer comfort to victims, families, and first responders.

Tina believes cats are uniquely suited for all kinds of therapy because they reach people in a way that humans cannot. In medical settings, people are often defensive and have their guard up when someone enters their room. Human health-care providers are at a natural disadvantage when they approach patients because they usually want to do something that makes people nervous, such as administer a test, perform a procedure, or give medication. But it's not that way with a cat. There's no need to put up one's guard because cats don't have an agenda. They don't have any prejudices; they just want to interact. Often when people see Basil, they're drawn to her because she's cute and has such an appealing personality. But Basil is clearly sensitive and intelligent beyond our understanding. Even Tina realizes this when she describes her role in Basil's work, "I'm just the chauffeur, she's the magic."

Basil
(Photo courtesy of Tina Parkhurst)

Chapter 15: Moe Grey, Educator and Celebrity Ambassador

I was a speaker at the Meow Meetup in Chicago when I met Moe Grey. He was heading toward the celebrity cat room with his caretaker, Prudence Bailey, and her sister, Christine. I was struck by his calm demeanor and charming personality. Moe Grey was more than happy to interact with me (and his many fans), so I asked about his story, which Prudence was delighted to share.

Moe Has Some Issues at His New Home

Prudence first learned about Moe when her dad told her that he had recently adopted a cat. Apparently, Moe's original companion had gone into a nursing home, so her dad agreed to take the cat. Prudence didn't think her dad had the experience or inclination to be a great caretaker, so she was concerned. She went over to her dad's apartment and felt as if she knew Moe from a dream. And when Moe saw her, he walked right over to her and sat in her lap. He strongly preferred Prudence over her sister and even her dad.

It wasn't long before problems began at her dad's house. Her father called and said Moe wasn't using his litterbox, and instead was urinating and defecating all over his clothing. Prudence thought Moe hadn't bonded with her father and that he might be missing his original caretaker, so she offered to adopt him. Prudence had the time and patience to help Moe. She reasoned he may not have used a litterbox before because he went outdoors to relieve himself. So the first thing she taught him was how to use a litterbox.

She went onto Facebook and researched different solutions to this problem. She routinely showed Moe his litterbox and rewarded him when he used it. It took a month for him to change his ways. Moe bonded strongly with Prudence; he would look into her eyes and seem to communicate, *you're my person*. He would not take food from anyone but her. Their relationship deepened.

Moe Goes on Facebook

About five months after Moe came to live with her, Prudence created a Facebook page for him so she could post a few photos. People started liking her page and she connected with other cat lovers through Facebook. Within a few months, he had thousands of followers. As of December 2022, he had over 47,000. He received all kinds of messages. One follower told Prudence that when she feels low, Moe helps make her day better. His fans have much to say about him.

> *"Moe Grey is one of the coolest cats out there—and no one looks as handsome in a bowtie as him. Love and purrs. Smooches"*

Visitors to his Facebook page often ask about his breed and what he eats, and they tell her about their current cats. Prudence isn't sure why her cat has so many followers. She hasn't done anything special with him—just posted photos and some short videos. People just seem to connect with him.

Cat Ambassador

Prudence has learned a lot from Moe. Her first discovery was how traumatic it can be to re-home a cat. She's explored the major issues that these cats face, such as litterbox problems, bonding, and trust issues. She's also investigated how to take the best care of her sweet cat, including what food is ideal for him, so she can help other cat caretakers.

Moe's popularity has led him to make visits to the public library and parks, where he's met kids of all ages. Apparently, he likes children, and they reciprocate the feeling. Kids often ask what the cat likes to do, what his favorite toy is, and how old he is. Moe has also helped Prudence's sister deal with anxiety and depression. Just being around Moe makes Christine feel better, alleviating her negative feelings. And at the Meow Meetup in Chicago, he met over one hundred fans. Several people gushed about how sweet, soft, and gentle he was after meeting him.

Moe Grey has had a large impact on Prudence by making her less shy and more outgoing with people. She takes Moe out on a leash, which invariably leads people to interact with them. She's made many new friends and has entered a world she never imagined. Moe's problems also spurred Prudence to do fundraisers for several cat shelters. She explained she wants to help cats and to educate people about the wonderful felines with whom we share our lives.

Moe Grey (Photo courtesy of Prudence Bailey)

Chapter 16: Nuala, Patient and Compassionate Healer

Nuala is a tortoiseshell cat who has "tortitude"—that diva-like attitude common to torties—according to her caretaker Mary Lu Meagher Chadwick. Nuala won't put up with any nonsense from the other three cats in her household, and she's clear when she needs her personal space or when another animal has crossed her boundary. She even has strong preferences on the route Mary Lu drives to familiar places. One day when they were in the car, Mary Lu took a different route home because there was an accident. As soon as they got off the main road, Nuala started meowing, showing her displeasure. When they returned to their regular route, she stopped. Talk about a backseat driver!

Nuala just "fell into therapy." Mary Lu saw how Nuala handled a variety of situations without any difficulty: she was accustomed to riding in a car, enjoyed meeting new people, and had no issues with loud noises. Everything came naturally to her. When Nuala was three years old, Mary Lu took her for the Pet Partner's test, and she passed easily, without any type of training. At age thirteen, Nuala began a well-deserved retirement. For ten years, however, she was a feline therapist extraordinaire.

A Decade of Cognitive, Physical, & Emotional Therapy

For eight years, Nuala was part of the Paws for Wellness program at Reading Hospital. She was the only cat on the animal-therapy team, and she made weekly visits to the Geriatric Psychiatric unit. The patients delighted in her company and fed her yogurt, her favorite treat. The elderly people who interacted with Nuala would often recall a pet they missed at home or one who had passed away. The visits were often emotional, and Nuala brought tears of joy or remembrance to these patients. Nuala always enjoyed interacting with the elderly, displaying tremendous patience with them.

She branched out into other areas of the hospital and spent time in the Brain Injury Unit. The patients in this ward suffered from a variety of traumatic brain injuries that made everyday tasks difficult. Nuala worked closely with a clinician and a dog team to help with memory activities. The therapist would tell the patient about Nuala and then ask, "what is the cat's name?" "What is the color of her leash?" "How old is the cat?" Then the therapist would ask similar questions about the dog.

Nuala also helped patients work on their fine-motor skills. A therapist would have the person perform various activities with the cat to facilitate coordination, such as brushing Nuala from head to tail or petting her in specific areas. Throughout these sessions, Nuala was patient and followed Mary Lu's directions closely.

Nuala made an impact on many people. One woman was in the stroke unit and was unable to talk, move, or make eye contact. But she loved cats. Mary Lu put Nuala next to her and explained that she was a therapy cat whose purpose was to help patients in the hospital. The woman didn't show much of a response, but the staff asked Mary Lu to bring Nuala back. The following day, the woman tracked the cat with her eyes and moved a little when Nuala was brought to her. And over the course of their time together, she eventually grabbed Nuala's leash. It was a huge step in her healing.

Adolescent Psychiatric Unit

Nuala was a big hit wherever she went in the hospital and many departments asked for her services. One invitation came from the Adolescent Psychiatric Unit, where groups of adolescents sat in a circle and took turns having Nuala sit on their laps while they pet her. One immigrant teenager wasn't sure about having a cat on her lap. She was anxious and fearful because she hadn't encountered pet felines before. Mary Lu explained she could just sit with the rest of the kids and watch Nuala. The next time she visited, Mary Lu asked if she wanted to touch Nuala's head. She did. And on the third visit, the girl asked to have Nuala on her lap, where she pet the cat with a huge smile on her face. The teen made a bold step overcoming her fear. It symbolized major progress for her.

Nuala was also great for the staff. They enjoyed seeing her and would stop to talk to her when she was at the hospital. As one staff member explained, "there were many days when Nuala's presence made my day better. And we always looked forward to seeing her in the unit."

Compassion

Mary Lu described Nuala as a complex and intelligent animal with tremendous compassion for her humans. When Mary Lu was diagnosed with breast cancer, Nuala stayed by her side day and night while she recovered. Nuala is a unique feline who has a gift she's shared with those who need physical or emotional healing. As Mary Lu explained to me:

> *"Our pets give so much to us. They can be companions, givers of unconditional love, and they support us emotionally. Pets who are involved in animal-therapy programs give so much to people they don't even know. Animals who are participating in Animal Assisted Interventions assist patients in the healing process both physically and emotionally. They truly offer a special gift."*

Mary Lu and Nuala
(Photo courtesy of Reading Hospital/Tower Health)

Chapter 17: Four Kittens Teach About Animal Advocacy and Courage

Charleen Propsom, who goes by Charlie, was walking her dog one cold September night when she noticed a black lump on the side of the road. It was an unusual shape, so she went to investigate it. That's when she realized it was a black cat who was hit by a car. And when she peered closer, she saw four kittens peeking out of the wreckage of the mother's body. She wanted to save them.

Charlie ran home, dropped off her dog, and grabbed some rubber gloves to pull the kittens out of their dead mother. The little creatures were tiny, and they made little mewing noises as she took them home. She called her veterinarian and asked about the "icky stuff" hanging off the babies, which she thought might be the mother's liver, mangled from the accident. The veterinarian patiently explained they were placentas, and that Charlie would have to tie off each kitten's umbilical cord. Charlie pulled out her mint dental floss and prayed the green color and mint flavoring wouldn't hurt the kittens. One by one they received their fancy mint tie-offs. Charlie then followed the vet's instructions to create a homemade kitten formula, which she gave them every two hours through some little doll bottles she found in her cupboard.

The four babies were unique. "Squeak" was a little grey kitten whose vocal tendencies earned him his name, while "Lady Guinevere" or Guinny was also grey but with subtle tabby stripes in her coat. "Chase" had the markings of a Holstein cow—black and white patches. And "Mickey," named after Mickey Mouse, was a glorious tuxedo cat with a white blaze on his forehead.

Charlie was unsure if the kittens would survive, but she decided to do anything she could to save them. She took them to work in a shopping bag so she could feed them every two hours. Several coworkers helped her with the feedings when she had meetings. And amazingly, because the kittens were so small, nobody even knew they were with her during the early weeks they went with her to work.

All was going well until Mickey got sick. He became lethargic, possibly because he went too long between feedings. Late in the workday, she and two coworkers rushed him to a veterinarian's office, where they learned his situation was grave. The vet recommended she euthanize him. Three grown women were standing in the lobby, quietly crying over his fate. Charlie asked if she didn't put him down what would happen. The vet said he would just go to sleep. If Mickey was going to die, Charlie wanted it to happen in the only home he had ever known. She made one small request, which was to inject Mickey with fluids. The vet didn't think it would make a difference, but Charlie persisted. Then she took the kitten home to let his fate unfold. She snuggled his tiny body next to his siblings, expecting him to die during the night. But a few hours later, all her kittens, including Mickey, were up and awake, scrambling for their next feeding. Mickey lived!

Caring for the kittens took a lot of energy over those eight weeks. Charlie went from a person who was unsure if she could save the little kittens to tending them, getting others to help, and advocating for them. Eventually the kittens could eat solid food and no longer needed to be bottle-fed. At that point, Charlie knew it was time to find homes for them. She placed each kitten with someone she personally knew. One woman at her office who had bottle fed the kittens adopted Squeak.

Charlie believes these kittens were a turning point in her life because they gave her the confidence that she could both care for and save animals. Charlie remembered the anguish of not being able to rescue every living creature around her when she was a child. Goldfish, cats, turtles, bunnies, and her sixteen-year-old dog were among the animals she tried to help and couldn't. Successfully raising the four kittens made her realize she could save the animals she felt so passionately about. She also discovered that one must advocate for those who have no voice. The day she told the veterinarian to give the kitten fluids and let it come home with her was a turning point that changed her.

Charlie founded Friends of Chicago Animal Care and Control (FCACC), which is a nonprofit group committed exclusively to saving the lives of the animals who come into the custody of Chicago Animal Care and Control (CACC). Each year, as many as seventeen thousand animals come through the doors of CACC because they're unwanted, lost, or abandoned. Most of these animals are wonderful, loving companion animals who have nowhere else to go. FCACC helps these animals by supplying food, medical care, and adoption opportunities.

Charlie believes her kitten experience taught her that if you push hard enough, you can accomplish amazing things. Saving the kittens who nearly became roadkill inspired Charlie to create a new program at FCACC called the After-Hours Crisis Care Program (AHCCP). The AHCCP takes sick and injured animals who come into the shelter after the veterinarians have left for the day and takes them to a private emergency clinic, where they receive life-saving care to stabilize them overnight. In the morning, they're transferred back to the shelter for further treatment. In its first couple of months, the program saved hundreds of dogs and cats who would have died.

I wish there were more people in the world like Charlie.

Anne E. Beall, PhD

(Image licensed from 123rf.com)

Chapter 18: Community Cats Create a Fierce Advocate Named Rae

Rae Bitner was never a cat person; she loved dogs. When she moved into her house, there were many feral cats outside. At first, she regarded them as a nuisance, but one cat family changed her beliefs and educated her about the plight of feral cats. It happened one night when she heard a crashing sound in her kitchen. When she entered the room, she saw that a mother cat had broken the screen on her kitchen window and carried her four kittens into the house. The whole family sat on the counter, eating some leftover bread. Rae realized they must have been starving because felines, being carnivores, prefer to eat meat. When she turned on the light, all the cats scampered out the back door—except for one little black kitten who fell into the sink. The kitten couldn't get out because the sink walls were too high.

Rae approached the kitten carefully because it was feral, and it growled at her. The mother cat and kittens were all waiting by the back door for their missing family member, and they peered in to see what would happen. Rae carefully wrapped the kitten in a towel and lifted it out of the sink before reuniting it with its family members. She watched them all trot into her yard.

She felt sorry for the hungry cats, so she put out some food and milk for them, which they ate at once. The next day, she bought some cat food and fed the little family regularly. And then one day the little kitten who had fallen into the sink didn't appear at mealtime. Rae wondered if something had happened, and she worried about their safety. A couple of weeks later, she saw the kittens on the busy street in front of her house. She wondered why they were on the street, so she went to check on them, and came upon a terrible scene. A car had hit the mother cat and the kittens didn't know what to do. They had nobody to take care of them.

Rae felt compelled to help, so she called the local humane society. They told her that a woman named Barb would come over the next day to help. When Barb arrived, she explained they would TNR the kittens (trap, neuter, and then return them) to Rae's yard so they wouldn't reproduce. She also brought houses for the kittens that could be placed in the yard.

Barb and Rae trapped the cats and got them fixed. All was going well, and the little family was being taken care of—they had a place to stay and regular food. Rae was proud of helping cats who had needed her so much.

Auto Accident

But then tragedy struck. Rae was in a jeep when a man in a van T-boned her after running a stop sign. His vehicle lifted her car off the ground, and it came down on its side many yards away. Rae had multiple fractures—including one to her back and neck. She could not walk for weeks. She also suffered a traumatic brain injury involving a midline shift, where the two front parts of her brain were overlapping. This led to stuttering and confused thinking. When she spoke, it was like reading from a book where there were pages missing. Entire memories were gone, and she had difficulty recalling simple things.

Rae loved her work as a warehouse manager but now could not stand or walk. Slight movements became excruciatingly painful. She could not return to her job. It was a depressing time. The one thing that buoyed her spirits was helping the cats. Even if she couldn't help herself, she wanted to make a difference for them.

She worked slowly and deliberately, given her injuries, and trapped other feral cats. By doing TNR in her neighborhood and then all over town, she could reduce the feral population. As of this writing, Rae has trapped and spayed/neutered hundreds of cats. And if any cats and kittens turned out to be friendly, she got them adopted. For the feral cats who remained outside, Rae set up caretakers for each cat colony. She educated the feeders about TNR and asked them to contact her if a new cat arrived in the area. And when she couldn't find a feeder, she took care of the colonies herself, paying for their food out of her own pocket. At one point, she took care of five colonies.

Cat Dumping

One day, a colony caretaker called Rae about a new cat who had shown up and was fighting with the other cats in her colony. This cat was unique because it was a Bengal cat—a purebred known for its distinctive spotted markings. It had obviously been someone's pet and was dumped or lost in the area.

Although the Bengal was friendly, he was so sick that Rae took him to her regular veterinarian for immediate care. The vet informed her that the cat was about fifteen years old and was starving. He had kidney disease, probably because of his malnourishment, and would probably die within a week.

Rae called him "Buddy" and adopted him so he could have a good end to his life. She gave him some CBD oil, and he gained weight and recovered his strength. He became an integral part of her family; her grandchildren loved to take him out for walks on a leash. He repaid Rae's kindness by showing how much he cared for her and everyone in the family. He only wanted to be with them and never asked to leave their house. Whenever he entered a room, he made his presence known. His personality was big. He lived another nine months.

Everyone in the household loved him, including her four Catahoula dogs, who usually disliked cats. On the day he passed, each dog took turns lying next to him in his last hours. Rae was surprised at how the dogs seemed to attend him as he took his leave from this world. "Animals have so much more knowledge than we give them credit for. Those dogs knew what was happening," she explained.

His fighting spirit and adoration taught Rae about persevering and advocating for those who cannot speak for themselves. "He taught me that you can't be bitter and that you have to keep trying to help those who need it, even when it's difficult." That lesson served her well in one situation, where she had to battle a couple who were throwing away a colony's food and water. She had video of the couple admitting they didn't like the cats and were removing their rations. Rae confronted them and told them she was trying to relocate the cats; but until then, they needed food and water. In Colorado where she lives, temperatures often reach over 100 degrees Fahrenheit, so water is important.

The couple has continued to thwart her efforts to help the cats, and she's shamed them on Facebook by revealing who they are and what they're doing. They're suing her for defamation of character and harassment, which she's fighting in court. She remains defiant. "You can't win a lawsuit for harassment and defamation if it's true," she said.

Community Cats on Facebook

Advocates for community cats number in the tens of thousands all over the world. Beth Frank has created a virtual community of these folks and runs over one hundred Facebook pages and groups dedicated to feral-cat advocates. Her most popular one is Trap Neuter Return Community,[x] (which has over 27,000 members). This group is a safe place for like-minded people who care about community cats. They can ask for help, get new ideas, share their successes (or failures), and find spay and neuter clinics. They have a fundraiser page, a petition page, and many specialty pages, such as a FIV and FeLV group dedicated to managing cats with these viruses. They also have rescue, foster, and adoption pages. When someone reaches out for assistance, the group members do whatever they can to help. One of Beth's groups is FixFinders,[xi] a database where one can enter a state and find low-cost spay-and-neuter clinics in that area. They also have a Community Cats United group for every state, where people can find local resources.

Beth saw the work that Rae was doing and asked if she'd be willing to be an administrator for some pages. At first, Rae said that she could only do things behind the scenes because she stutters as a result of the accident. But over time, she's become the Director of Operations and the Treasurer on the board for Community Cats United, Inc. She oversees all state groups and many of the Facebook pages and will often reach out to people who are looking for resources. Rae also speaks to city officials in many states to help them set up

TNR programs within their area. And she even gives radio and newspaper interviews about TNR. She discovered that when she talked about feral cats, a subject she knows a lot about, she didn't stutter. In fact, when I interviewed her for this chapter, she didn't stutter once. As she explained to me, "God puts us where we need to be. This is what I was meant to do."

Community Cat
The tipped left ear indicates the animal has been spayed or neutered
(Image licensed from 123rf.com)

Chapter 19: Ayla and Buddy, Life Coaches

I've known Debbie Gleason for over thirty years; we met in high school. In those days, she was a vivacious, beautiful strawberry blonde who looked her best every day with makeup, dresses, and high-heeled shoes. She had a lot of energy and always had a quick comeback for everyone. Years later, she told me how much her cats have helped her.

There are some people in this world who are born with every advantage. Debbie wasn't one of them. Her mother was only sixteen when she gave birth to Debbie. As a result, Debbie was raised sometimes by her mother, sometimes by her grandmother and grandfather, but largely by herself. Her father was a heroin addict who was absent from her life early on. She wanted to have a relationship with him, and when she was sixteen, her father promised to take her out to dinner and buy her some Christmas gifts. Debbie got all dressed up and waited by the window for him. He never showed. A few years later, he died of a heroin overdose.

Debbie's mother had her own difficulties and ended up marrying a violent man who often screamed and hit his wife. One day, he smashed Debbie's stereo and dresser in a fit of rage. She ran away in the middle of winter without warm clothing and ended up walking along a lonely road. When some men pulled up in a car asking if she needed help, she was happy to get out of the cold. They offered to take her to get something to eat and wear.

They took her to a house where they all had a big spaghetti dinner. When the men offered her wine, she declined, but they continued to press her. Eventually, she drank some wine to please her hosts. It wasn't long afterward that she felt sick. She blacked out and then the men took her clothes, put her in a bedroom, and locked the door. They wouldn't let her out. Debbie was terrified. And then they raped her repeatedly. When she resisted, they beat her mercilessly. They held Debbie against her will for over two days. Despite her tears and requests to go, they were clear: she was not leaving.

Debbie knew the men would kill her. She developed an incredible strength and resolve to escape. Eventually, she climbed out of the window and jumped to safety. And that's when she ran and ran and ran. It was nighttime in a deserted area, and she was alone. She finally flagged down a car whose driver took her to the nearest police station. She was safe.

Debbie was examined at a rape-crisis center, where they encouraged her to press charges. Rape survivors often don't want to relive their trauma by going through a trial; many teenagers wouldn't have had the emotional fortitude. Debbie didn't want anyone else to have her experience, so she forged ahead. She was terrified as she sat in court and identified her rapists. They received a two-year prison sentence. They long ago served their time, but Debbie has lived in an emotional prison of fear and trauma since that day.

There are different ways that people cope with traumatic experiences. Some people turn to family and friends, others find religion, and many people cope with alcohol and drugs. Debbie turned to "partying" to help lessen her pain. Always a fun person, she saw alcohol as something that made her even more entertaining. The girl who didn't drink became the woman who could drink you under the table.

Debbie had a lovely singing voice and she hoped to have a career as a singer. She regularly performed with many bands in Worcester, Massachusetts, and she wanted to go to New York City, where she had connections that could lead to an actual career in music. But her grandmother, her only genuine support, begged her not to go. Debbie was torn, but eventually stayed in Worcester because she didn't want to lose her one lifeline. She went to school for fashion merchandising and design and then attended drawing classes at the Boston Art Institute. But these early years were the beginning of a downward slide.

Debbie's life hasn't turned out as she wished, and she blames herself. She's harder on herself than she should be. Most people who grow up with these kinds of disadvantages and painful experiences don't remain unaffected. Interestingly, Debbie has channeled a lot of her energy into helping others, particularly stray animals.

Debbie has adopted and cared for several stray cats over the years. Several of them were sick when they came into her life. They seem to find her when they need a place to stay and someone to care for them. But the cats offer much more in return; they provide Debbie with love and appreciation. Debbie feels that her cats have truly taught her she has value and that her life has meaning.

Her current cat, Ayla, is so bonded to her she senses Debbie's every mood. When Debbie is sad, Ayla is there for her. Debbie feels the cat constantly lets her know how much she loves her. And when Debbie had surgery, Ayla was with her around the clock. She placed herself on top of Debbie, as if to keep her in bed and comfort her. Ayla seemed to communicate that Debbie needed to heal and that she was there to protect her and keep her safe.

Another feline presence in Debbie's life was a black male cat named Buddy, who was so bonded to her he followed her everywhere. Buddy was an indoor-outdoor cat who whined incessantly to go out. One day, he went outside and didn't return. Debbie watched and waited, hoping he would come back. After four weeks, he finally reappeared. He gave Debbie hope and demonstrated that miracles are possible. He also showed he wouldn't abandon her.

Debbie has had many challenges including unemployment, illness, and surgeries. But despite all she's endured, she's hopeful—just like that plucky, pretty, redheaded girl from high school. I asked her how she's managed, given everything that has happened, and she replied, "there is a lot of good in this world, and a lot of love. Just look at my cats."

Chapter 20: Survey of How Cats Help Americans and Prevalent Attitudes

To understand the role that cats play in Americans' lives, we conducted a survey of a representative sample of the U.S. population. We surveyed 1,507 people in 2020 who have lived with a cat, either currently or as an adult. We asked them to tell us about the favorite cats in their lives and what they felt about each one. We also asked about their attitudes toward stray and feral cats.

My firm, Beall Research Inc., conducts qualitative and quantitative research for Fortune 500 companies. We conduct surveys on a variety of topics, although not usually on cats. Below are the findings from this study.

Cats in the Home

Among adults who have lived with a cat, over three-fifths of them currently have a cat and over half have a dog. Other pets, such as ferrets, mice, birds, and rabbits, are rarer.

N = 1,507	Percentage
Cat	61%
Dog	55%
Rabbit	2%
Parrot or parakeet	2%
Other type of bird	2%
Ferret	1%
Guinea Pig	1%
Hamster	1%

Iguana or Lizard	1%
Mouse	1%
Rat	0%
None of the above	17%

Table 1: Current pets in the home

Approximately 8 in 10 respondents currently live with 1-2 cats in their household.

N = 914	Percentage
1 cat	53%
2 cats	30%
3 cats	8%
4 cats	4%
5 or more cats	5%

Table 2: Number of cats currently in the household

Over half (55%) of respondents have had 1-2 cats as an adult and the rest have had 3 or more cats during their adult years.

N = 1,507	Percentage
1 cat	29%
2 cats	26%
3 cats	11%
4 cats	9%
5 cats	7%
6 or more cats	18%

Table 3: Number of cats that respondents have had as an adult

Communication and Intelligence

We asked survey respondents to tell us about one to three favorite cats they've had as an adult. Approximately 60% of the cats that respondents described were currently living with them at the time of the survey. There were 1,507 respondents who answered questions about 3,169 cats. Thus, we could understand over 3,000 cats and over 3,000 cat-human relationships. We asked several questions about each cat: how close the person felt to each feline, how much communication occurred, and in what ways the cat and the person had helped one another.

The first question we asked was how intelligent each cat is compared to other animals. As you can see in the below figure, two-thirds of these cats are extremely intelligent compared to other animals.

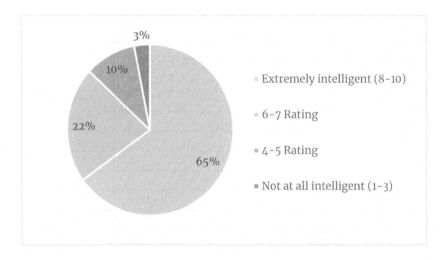

Figure 1: Intelligence of cat compared to other animals (n=3,169)

We then asked how intelligent the cat is compared to humans, and one-third of these favorite cats are extremely intelligent relative to people.

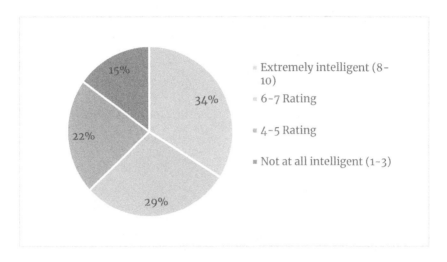

Figure 2: Intelligence of cat compared to humans (n=3,169)

We also asked how much communication occurs between the caretaker and the cat, and we learned that over half (59%) of these relationships have a tremendous amount of communication. Only 4% have no communication.

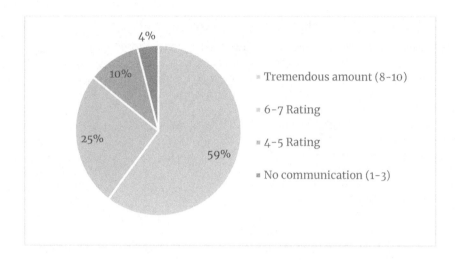

Figure 3: Amount of communication between caretaker & cat (n=3,169)

When asked how well the cats read their caretaker's feelings and preferences, over half of these cats appear to read the person extremely well. This finding is not in line with stereotypes of cats as aloof and disinterested. Only 4% of cats did not read their caretaker well at all.

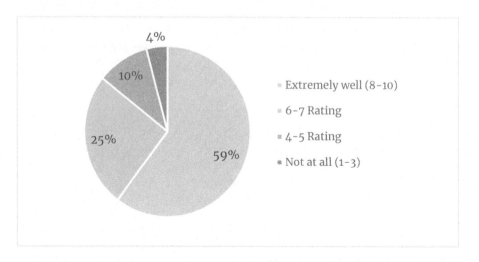

Figure 4: How well the cat reads the caretaker (n=3,169)

Given that communication is a two-way street, we inquired how well the caretaker reads the feelings and preferences of the cat. Apparently, it's similar to how well the cat reads the person. Caretakers appear to read their cats well, as shown in Figure 5.

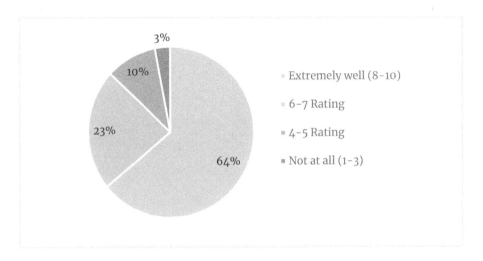

Figure 5: How well caretaker reads the cat (n=3,169)

We found that the amount of communication between the caretaker and cat is highly correlated with how well the cat and person read one another, as well as the level of closeness with the cat. Thus, both talking to your cat and listening to their communications leads to greater closeness and a greater ability to read the feline.

Relationship & Helping

We then asked how close the person feels to each cat. Given the amount of communication that occurs between cats and caretakers, it's not surprising that over three-quarters (77%) feel extremely close to the cat.

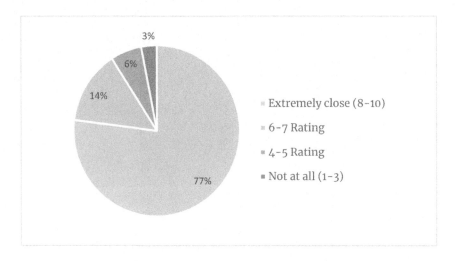

Figure 6: How close the caretaker feels to cat (n=3,169)

We also learned that over half (56%) spend 6-23 hours a day with the cat.

N = 3,169	Percentage
24 hours a day	13%
12-23 hours each day	25%
6-11 hours each day	31%
3-5 hours each day	17%
1-2 hours each day	8%
Less than 1 hour per day	6%

Table 4: Hours spent each day with cat

We were curious how people help their cats, so we provided a list of common ways that people assist cats and asked if they had helped their cat in any of these ways. Interestingly, playing with the cat and providing them with companionship and comfort were among the top ways that the person helped a cat. These responses suggest that the human-cat bond is strong, and that people are doing things they feel their cat appreciates.

N = 3,169	Percentage
I played with him/her	87%
I cared for him/her daily	84%
I provided him/her with companionship	79%
I comforted him/her when needed	72%
I cared for the animal when he/she was sick	60%
I gave him/her medicine	52%
I saved his/her life by adopting from a shelter	28%
I cared for the animal when he/she lost another animal	17%
I saved him/her from an abusive situation	16%
I cared for the animal when he/she lost a human	9%
I gave him/her physical therapy	7%
None of the above	1%

Table 5: How the caretaker has helped cat

We also asked how the cat had helped them and the most common response was that the cat made the person happy, cat provided companionship, loved their caretaker unconditionally, was a friend, or was someone whom they could cuddle or hug.

N = 3,169	Percentage
He/she made me feel happy	72%
He/she provided me with companionship	68%
He/she loved me unconditionally	65%
He/she provided me with friendship	64%
He/she gave me someone to hug or cuddle	61%
He/she comforted me when I needed it	56%
Being around him/her made me feel better about the world	54%
He/she made me feel needed	53%
He/she was someone I could talk to	44%
He/she helped me when I was having difficulty emotionally	41%
He/she made me feel better about myself	36%
He/she gave me a purpose	33%
He/she made me feel proud	31%
He/she helped me cope with anxiety, PTSD, or depression	30%
He/she gave me someone to live for	25%
He/she helped me through an illness	19%
He/she got me through a death or divorce	16%
He/she was a substitute for a child	16%
He/she helped me concentrate	15%
He/she got me through a difficult work situation	15%
He/she protected me physically	12%
He/she got me to go out of the house	11%
He/she helped me do something I was afraid to do	8%
None of the above	3%

Table 6: How cat has helped caretaker

We wanted to understand how the caretaker felt about the cat. About two-thirds of respondents reported that they like the cat's personality, regard them as a family member, and that this creature is an important part of their life.

N = 3,169	Percentage
I enjoy his/her personality	67%
I regard him/her as a family member	64%
He/she is an important part of my life	60%
I like that he/she is independent and doesn't require as much care as a dog	48%
Life would be empty without him/her	42%
I regard him/her as one of my children	37%
He/she makes me feel special	33%
I've learned a lot from him/her	32%
He/she is my best friend	31%
I'm a better person because of him/her	30%
He/she made me feel differently about cats	30%
He/she connects with me more strongly than most humans	28%
He/she understands me better than most humans	26%
He/she connects with me more strongly than any other animal ever did	23%
He/she made me feel differently about animals	21%
I regard him/her as a pet, not a family member	10%
None of the above	2%

Table 7: Feelings about cat

Indoor and outdoor cats

We asked how many cats in the respondents' households are indoors all the time and how many of the cats go outside. Apparently in one in three indoor cats in U.S. households goes outside.

N = 1,507	
Number cats in your household who **live indoors 100%** of the time	1.44 (67%)
Number of cats in your household who **live indoors and go outside**	.7 (33%)
TOTAL INDOOR CATS	2.14 cats

Table 8: Average number and percentage of indoor cats

Given that this survey is a representative sample of Americans with cats, we can **estimate the number of indoor cats (even those who go outside) is approximately 112 million.**

We also asked how many cats **live outdoors** on each person's property. We defined **feral cats** as cats that are born in the wild. They are different from **stray cats**, which are pet cats that have been lost or abandoned and were not born in the wild. The two types of cats look the same.

Apparently stray/feral cats are common. One-third of the stray/feral cats outdoors are being fed regularly. About one-quarter of outdoor cats are part of the household as shown in Table 9.

N = 1,507	
Number of **stray or feral cats** on your property **whom you do not feed**	.62 (41%)
Number of **stray or feral cats** on your property **whom you feed regularly**	.53 (35%)
Number of cats in your household who live outside 100% of the time **that you feed and that are not stray or feral cats**	.36 (24%)
TOTAL OUTDOOR CATS	1.52 cats

Table 9: Average number and percentage of outdoor cats

Given that this survey is a representative sample of Americans with cats, we can **estimate the number of outdoor cats is approximately 79 million.**

We asked if the respondents currently have a feral cat colony that they regularly feed. We defined a feral cat colony as a group of feral cats that lives in a single place for a long period.

N = 1,507	Percentage
Yes, I have a feral cat colony I regularly feed	8%
No, I do not	92%

Table 10: Feral cat colony that is regularly fed

Almost half of colony caretakers (47%) have 1-3 outdoor cats in their colony.

N = 119	Percentage
1 cat	17%
2 cats	12%
3 cats	18%
4 cats	11%
5 cats	17%
6 or more cats	25%

Table 11: Number of cats in colony

We asked how much the person is spending on feeding the cats each month and over half (56%) are spending $10 to $49 per month—$120 to $588 per year.

N = 296[1]	Percentage
$0	14%
$1-$9 per month	8%
$10-$24 per month	36%
$25-$49 per month	21%
$50 or more per month	21%

Table 12: Amount spent feeding colony cats per month

---

[1] Base is those who feed strays/feral cats, not just self-identified colony caretakers

Why did the person start taking care of stray cats? The two most common reasons were because they felt sorry for them or because they saw a kitten or cat outside who was hungry.

N =296[2]	Percentage
I felt sorry for them	68%
I saw kittens or a cat outside who were hungry	59%
I saw kittens or a cat who was hurt	24%
I had a neighbor who was feeding them	20%
A group of people was trying to get rid of the cats	13%
I learned about stray/feral cats from an organization	13%
I learned about stray/feral cats from a friend/family member	13%
I learned about stray/feral cats from a book, magazine, newspaper, television show/news report, etc.	10%
I wanted to reduce the number of them	7%
I had an indoor cat who became an outdoor cat who had kittens	6%

Table 13: Reasons caretaker started taking care of stray cats

Approximately 1 in 10 colony caretakers said they have been harassed, and 2 in 10 said that people had complained about them taking care of the cats.

N = 296	Percentage
Yes, I have been harassed	11%
No, but some people have complained	19%
No, I have not been harassed	70%

Table 14: Whether caretaker has been harassed

---

[2] Base is those who feed strays/feral cats, not just self-identified colony caretakers

General Attitudes toward Stray Cats and Euthanasia

The three most common feelings about stray cats were that the person felt sorry for them, wished they could help them, and tried to help stray cats when possible.

N = 1,507	Percentage
I feel sorry for them	63%
I wish I could help them	53%
I try to help them when I can	51%
I don't mind them	40%
I don't have any feelings about stray cats	6%
I consider them to be pests	5%
I consider them to be dangerous	4%
I am afraid of them	3%
I hate stray cats	2%

Table 15: Feelings about stray cats

We then gave a hypothetical situation and asked what respondents would do if they saw a stray cat in their community and could only choose between two courses of action—leaving the cat outside where it is or having the cat caught and then put down—which would they consider to be the more humane option for the cat? Most people would leave the cat where it is.

N = 1,507	Percentage
Leave the cat where it is	78%
Have the cat put down	7%
Don't know	15%

Table 16: Actions toward stray cats

We then asked if they knew that the stray cat was going to *die in two years* because it would be hit by a car, which option they would consider the most humane. About half said they would leave the cat where it is, and one quarter didn't know what to do.

N = 1,507	Percentage
Leave the cat where it is and let it live two years before dying	53%
Have the cat put down	12%
Adopt it/take it in and care for it	5%
Get help from someone/call a shelter/find it a good home	5%
Don't know	24%

Table 17: Actions toward stray cat that will die in two years

We asked how people felt about euthanizing cats at pet shelters and the majority believe that cats should only be euthanized when they're either too ill or too aggressive to be adopted.

N = 1,507	Percentage
I believe that shelters should put down cats when there are too many of them	9%
I believe that shelters should only put down cats when they are either too ill or too aggressive to be adopted	66%
I don't believe that shelters should ever put down cats	24%

Table 18: Attitudes toward euthanizing cats in shelters

Attitudes toward TNR

In the next questions we asked about attitudes toward Trap-Neuter-Return (TNR) programs. Below are the description and definitions we used.

> *Some of the cats you see outside are **feral cats**. Feral cats are cats that are born in the wild. They are different from **stray cats**, which are pet cats that have been lost or abandoned and were not born in the wild. The two types of cats do not look different. There is a program to help feral cats. It's called the **Trap-Neuter-Return** (TNR) program. With TNR programs, feral cats are humanely trapped and then spayed/neutered so they can't have kittens. After they have recovered from surgery, they are relocated or returned to their original location.*
>
> *This program stabilizes and reduces feral cat populations. The behaviors associated with mating, such as yowling, spraying, and fighting, stop after cats are spayed/neutered.*

We asked whether respondents had heard of TNR before the survey and about half said they had not heard about it. The number of Americans who are familiar with TNR has increased since we first surveyed them in 2013[xii]. At that time, about 71% of pet owners had never heard of TNR and only 5% were very familiar with it. Thus, it appears Americans have become more familiar with TNR programs over the past seven years.

N = 1,507	Percentage
I had not heard of this program	52%
I had heard of it but **didn't know much about it**	19%
I have heard of it and **knew something about it**	18%
I have heard of it and am **very familiar with it**	11%

Table 19: Knowledge of Trap-Neuter-Return programs

We asked how people regard TNR programs and two-thirds of respondents are extremely positive about them. Only 4% of those surveyed have an extremely negative perception of these programs

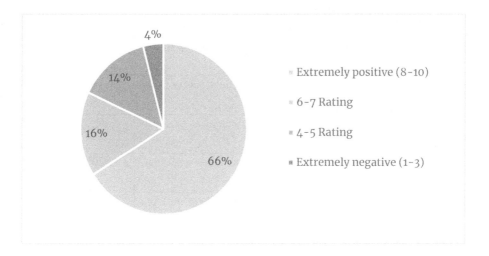

Figure 7: How respondents view TNR programs (n=1,507)

We then asked about the importance of specific information about TNR. Most of the information is perceived as important. The items with the highest endorsement are that the cats are regularly vaccinated, that TNR programs stabilize and reduce the number of feral cats, and that the cats are monitored for diseases and are not a health hazard.

N = 1,507	(% Rating 8, 9, or 10)
Cats in TNR programs are regularly vaccinated and are not at risk to transmit rabies or other feline diseases to other cats	71%
TNR programs have been shown to stabilize and reduce feral-cat populations	69%
Cats in TNR programs are monitored for diseases and have not been shown to be a health hazard	69%
Cats in TNR programs are less likely to fight (because they have been spayed/neutered) and they are less likely to be injured by other cats	65%
Local humane societies monitor feral cat colonies and ensure they are being properly cared for	65%
Cats in TNR programs live in urban, suburban, and rural areas and have been effective at reducing the number of rats in those areas	64%
Cats who are part of TNR programs have been successfully used to get rid of rats and mice	64%
Cats in TNR programs are shown to live as long as cats who are indoors	62%
Local humane societies are generally the ones who trap, neuter, and return/relocate the cats	60%
Cats in TNR programs belong in a colony where they are regularly fed by a colony caretaker and therefore do not have to hunt for their food	55%
Cats in TNR programs are fed by a caretaker and are similar in size and weight to indoor cats	55%
Cats in TNR programs do not significantly reduce bird populations	47%

Table 20: Information about TNR programs

We asked which information was **most** important, and learned that regular vaccinations, low transmission of diseases and the stabilization/reduction of feral-cat populations are most important.

N = 1,507	(% select most important)
Cats in TNR programs are regularly vaccinated and are not at risk to transmit rabies or other feline diseases to other cats	18%
TNR programs have been shown to stabilize and reduce feral-cat populations	17%
Local humane societies monitor feral cat colonies and ensure they are being properly cared for	14%
Cats in TNR programs are monitored for diseases and have not been shown to be a health hazard	8%
Cats in TNR programs are shown to live as long as cats who are indoors	7%
Cats in TNR programs belong in a colony where they are regularly fed by a colony caretaker and therefore do not have to hunt for their food	7%
Cats in TNR programs live in urban, suburban, and rural areas and have been effective at reducing the number of rats in those areas	7%
Cats who are part of TNR programs have been successfully used to get rid of rats and mice	6%
Cats in TNR programs are less likely to fight (because they have been spayed/neutered) and they are less likely to be injured by other cats	5%
Local humane societies are generally the ones who trap, neuter, and return/relocate the cats	5%
Cats in TNR programs do not significantly reduce bird populations	3%
Cats in TNR programs are fed by a caretaker and are similar in size and weight to indoor cats	3%

Table 21: Most important information about TNR programs

After being given this information, we asked how respondents felt about TNR programs. We discovered that they are generally more positive about them, with 78% reporting that they feel extremely positive about them. In the initial question, 66% were extremely positive before they learned more about these programs.

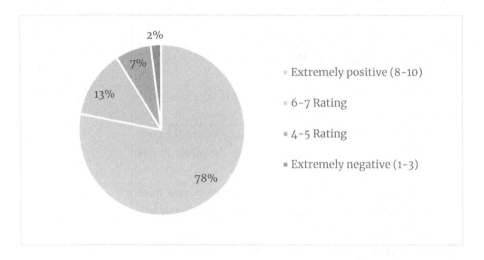

Figure 8: How respondents feel about TNR after information (n=1,507)

We also asked how believable the information was that was presented. Table 22 shows the most believable information is that TNR programs reduce/stabilize the feral cat populations, reduce rodents in areas where they live, and local humane societies are the ones who trap, neuter and return/relocate the cats.

N =1,507	(% Rating 8, 9, or 10)
TNR programs have been shown to stabilize and reduce feral-cat populations	64%
Cats in TNR programs live in urban, suburban, and rural areas and have been effective at reducing the number of rats in those areas	60%
Local humane societies are generally the ones who trap, neuter, and return/relocate the cats	60%
Cats who are part of TNR programs have been successfully used to get rid of rats and mice	59%
Cats in TNR programs are regularly vaccinated and are not at risk to transmit rabies or other feline diseases to other cats	58%
Cats in TNR programs are monitored for diseases and have not been shown to be a health hazard	57%
Cats in TNR programs are less likely to fight (because they have been spayed/neutered) and they are less likely to be injured by other cats	56%
Local humane societies monitor feral cat colonies and ensure they are being properly cared for	53%
Cats in TNR programs are shown to live as long as cats who are indoors	48%
Cats in TNR programs belong in a colony where they are regularly fed by a colony caretaker and therefore do not have to hunt for their food	48%
Cats in TNR programs are fed by a caretaker and are similar in size and weight to indoor cats	49%
Cats in TNR programs do _not_ significantly reduce bird populations	42%

Table 22: Believability of information about TNR programs

When asked if there were a free Trap-Neuter-Return program in their area, how likely they would be to support such a program, about two-thirds said they would be extremely likely.

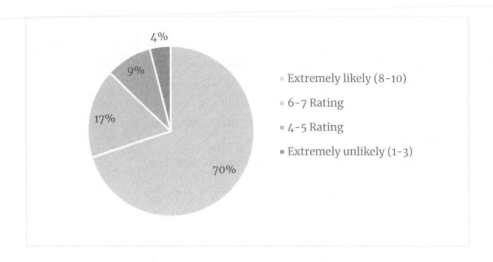

Figure 9: How likely to support a free TNR program (n=1,507)

We asked how likely respondents would be to become a colony caretaker if there were a Trap-Neuter-Return program in their area. Approximately one-third said they would be extremely likely to become a caretaker.

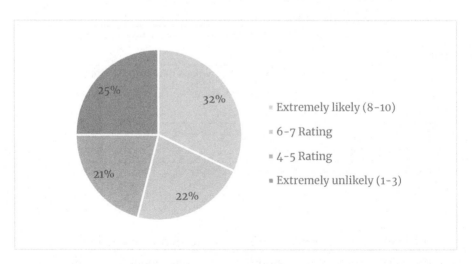

Figure 10: How likely to become a colony caretaker (n=1,388)

Demographics of Survey Respondents

The demographics of the survey respondents are like the U.S. population. Most respondents for this survey were between the ages of 30 and 59.

N = 1,507	Percentage
18-29 years of age	14%
30-39	19%
40-49	20%
50-59	20%
60-69	19%
70-79	8%

Table 23: Age of respondents

Slightly more females than males either currently or previously had a cat as an adult.

N = 1,507	Percentage
Males	47%
Females	53%

Table 24: Gender of respondents

Most respondents are white/Caucasian.

N = 1,507	Percentage
White or Caucasian	84%
Hispanic or Latino	7%
African American or Black	8%
Asian	2%
Native American or Alaskan Native	2%
Native Hawaiian or other Pacific Islander	0%
Some other ethnicity	0%

Table 25: Race/ethnicity of respondents

Most respondents have an annual income of between $25,000-$74,000

N = 1,507	Percentage
Less than $10,000	6%
$10,000 - $14,999	7%
$15,000 - $24,999	11%
$25,000 - $34,999	17%
$35,000 - $49,999	15%
$50,000 – $74,999	19%
$75,000 - $99,999	9%
$100,000 - $149,999	8%
$150,000 - $199,999	3%
$200,000 or more	2%
Prefer not to answer	3%

Table 26: Annual household income of respondents

Respondents are distributed around the country in a similar proportion to the overall general population.

N = 1,507	Percentage
Northeast (CT, MA, ME, NH, NJ, NY, PA, RI, VT)	16%
Midwest (IA, IL, IN, KS, MI, MN, MO, ND, NE, OH, SD, WI)	22%
South (AL, AR, DC, DE, FL, GA, KY, LA, MD, MS, NC, OK, SC, TN, TX, VA, WV)	39%
West (AK, AZ, CA, CO, HI, ID, MT, NM, NV, OR, UT, WA, WY)	23%

Table 27: Region of the country where respondents lived

Three-fifths of respondents do not have a child currently living in their home.

N = 1,507	Percentage
None	60%
1	15%
2	15%
3	7%
4	2%
5 or more	1%

Table 28: Number of children living at home

Almost half of people live in a suburban area or small city.

N = 1,507	Percentage
Urban/Large city	26%
Suburban/Small city	45%
Rural/Small town	30%

Table 29: Area where respondent lived

Anne E. Beall, PhD.

Anne E. Beall is an animal advocate who has written extensively about the human-animal bond. She is an award-winning author whose books have been featured in *People Magazine*, *Chicago Tribune*, *Toronto Sun*, *Hers Magazine*, *Ms. Career Girl*, and she's been interviewed by NBC, NPR, and WGN. Her book, *Cinderella Didn't Live Happily Ever After,* won a Gold Award from Literary Titan and her book, *Heartfelt Connections,* was named one of the top 100 Indy books by *Shelf Unbound.*

Beall received her MS, MPhil, and PhD degrees in social psychology from Yale University and is the founder of the strategic market-research firm, Beall Research. In her spare time, she explores the many restaurants of the city, and runs along the lakefront.

Steve Dale

Steve Dale, CABC (certified animal behavior consultant) is the author of a popular blog, www.stevedalepetworld.com. He is host of two national radio shows, and is heard on WGN Radio, Chicago.

His many TV appearances include Oprah to National Geographic Explorer. He's a contributor on syndicated "HouseSmarts TV."

He's a columnist for *Veterinary Practice News*, and contributing editor *CATSTER* magazine. He edited "Decoding Your Dog," authored by American College of Veterinary Behaviorists, and authored the foreword of "Decoding Your Cat." He's contributed to dozens of books and publications, including veterinary books, "The Cat: Clinical Medicine and Management" and "Treatment and Care of the Geriatric Veterinary Patient."

Steve speaks around the world at animal behavior and veterinary conferences. He's a speaker for Fear Free and also Cat Friendly Practices. He serves of the Boards of the Winn Feline Foundation, the Human Animal Bond Association and Veterinary Professionals Against Puppy Mills, which he co-founded, as serves on several advisory boards. He's a co-founder of the CATaylst Council, also past board member American Humane Association.

His many awards and honors include the AVMA Humane Award, and he was inducted in the Dog Writer's Association Hall of Fame.

End Notes

i https://www.sciencenews.org/article/cats-attachment-styles-people

ii https://petpartners.org/about-us/

iii https://www.lolatherescuedcat.com/p/our-book.html

iv https://www.lolatherescuedcat.com/

v https://www.youtube.com/watch?v=T0rbvgUnaj4&feature=youtu.be

vi https://www.youtube.com/watch?v=p5w0jTYNJzE&feature=youtu.be

vii www.spacecatacademy.com

viii https://www.facebook.com/Help-save-Belleville-cats-Belleville-NJ-07109-109336053959808

ix https://www.facebook.com/groups/14792834056728 36/

x https://www.facebook.com/TrapNeuterReturnCommunityCCU

xi https://www.communitycatsunited.org/fixfinder

xii Beall, 2019, (originally published in 2014). Community Cats: A Journey Into the World of Feral Cats. Chicago: Beall Research. https://www.amazon.com/Community-Cats-Journey-World-Feral/dp/179685719X/ref=sr_1_2?dchild=1&keywords=beall+community+cats&qid=1588259236&sr=8-2

Made in the USA
Monee, IL
19 March 2024

54728948R00080